SHAWN THORNTON
FIGHTING MY WAY TO THE TOP

Shawn Thornton
with Dale Arnold

TRIUMPH
BOOKS

Library of Congress Cataloging-in-Publication Data

Names: Thornton, Shawn, author. | Arnold, Dale, author.
Title: Shawn Thornton : fighting my way to the top / Shawn Thornton with Dale Arnold.
Other titles: Fighting my way to the top
Description: Chicago, Illinois : Triumph Books, [2021]
Identifiers: LCCN 2021026465 | ISBN 9781629378671 (hardcover) | ISBN 9781641256940 (epub)
Subjects: LCSH: Thornton, Shawn. | Hockey players—Canada—Biography. | Hockey players—United States—Biography.
Classification: LCC GV848.5.T55 A3 2021 | DDC 796.962092 [B]—dc23
LC record available at https://lccn.loc.gov/2021026465

This book is available in quantity at special discounts for your group or organization. For further information, contact:

Triumph Books LLC
814 North Franklin Street
Chicago, Illinois 60610
(312) 337-0747
www.triumphbooks.com

Printed in U.S.A.
ISBN: 978-1-62937-867-1
Design by Patricia Frey
Page production by Nord Compo
Photos courtesy of Shawn Thornton unless otherwise indicated

To my daughters, Nora and Ainsley, and the people who helped me along the way: my wife, Erin; parents, Mark and Christine; grandparents, Gerald, Doreen, Maureen, and Harry; my coach and mentor, Lionel; and all my teammates, coaches, and friends.

—S.T.

My thanks to Shawn, for trusting me to help tell his story, and to Triumph Books for the opportunity. As always, my thanks to my wife, Susan; and kids, Taylor, Alysha, and Brianna, for their continuing support and encouragement.

—D.A.

CONTENTS

FOREWORD *by Tuukka Rask*   **vii**

PROLOGUE   **xiii**

CHAPTER 1.   Of John Wayne and Boom Boom Shamoon   **1**

CHAPTER 2.   Turning Pro   **17**

CHAPTER 3.   Bird Dog and the Rock   **33**

CHAPTER 4.   From Winter to Summer   **45**

CHAPTER 5.   Michel, Montreal, and Me   **57**

CHAPTER 6.   Shipping Up to Boston   **71**

CHAPTER 7.   The Pittsburgh Penguins and Me   **91**

CHAPTER 8.   The Collapse   **101**

CHAPTER 9.   2010–11 Season   **107**

CHAPTER 10.   The Merlot Line   **117**

CHAPTER 11.   My Buddy Tuukka   **127**

CHAPTER 12.   Highlight   **137**

CHAPTER 13.   An Identity Is Born   145

CHAPTER 14.   The Run to the Cup   153

CHAPTER 15.   My Day(s) with the Cup   177

CHAPTER 16.   The List   187

CHAPTER 17.   The Elephant in the Room   199

CHAPTER 18.   The Next Step   213

CHAPTER 19.   Giving Back   227

CHAPTER 20.   Changing Careers   243

EPILOGUE   251

FOREWORD

I WAS 19 YEARS OLD, and I didn't know anyone or anything. The Toronto Maple Leafs had traded my rights in June 2006 to the Boston Bruins for former Rookie of the Year Andrew Raycroft. It was fall 2007 and not only was I making the move from my native Finland to North America, but I was making the move to professional hockey and would spend the season playing for the Providence Bruins of the American Hockey League. It was my first pro training camp, and I was a little nervous.

Shawn Thornton was also in his first training camp with the Bruins after signing in the off-season as a free agent, but he was a veteran and had already played in more than 200 professional games and had won the Stanley Cup with the Anaheim Ducks. He and I were on opposite ends of the experience spectrum, and I had no reason to expect he would give me the time of day. That was because I hadn't met him yet.

Shawn went out of his way to introduce himself and help me whenever he could. I didn't even know where I could go to get a bite to eat away from the rink, and Shawn took me under his wing. He taught me how to handle myself away from the rink, and that's how we started bonding. And now we've been friends for more than 13 years.

I would learn, through the years, that this was simply who Shawn was. I can't tell you how many times Shawn and his wife, Erin, would invite players over to their place for a meal and a conversation, especially around any holiday. If you were alone in Boston and it was a holiday, you were made a member of the Thornton family.

It's safe to say people's personalities are different on the ice and off the ice. Thorty was always an enforcer on the ice and fought for his teammates. I was the goalie who was supposed to stay calm and quiet when I was playing. Now don't get me wrong; I was a lot more emotional on the ice early in my career. That desire to win was driving me nuts, and through experience I learned to channel that energy. But when you're 19 years old and playing on a Sunday afternoon in Providence, you don't understand that. Sometimes you have to learn the hard way.

I know how strange it sounds that a quiet goalie from Finland and a not-so-quiet tough guy from Ontario would become friends, but we just did. He was that kind of guy. I played four games in Boston in 2007–08 and only one in the 2008–09 season, but I finally made the permanent move to the NHL in the fall of 2009, and Shawn was always my friend.

When you're playing in goal, you get to see everyone on the ice in front of you, and Shawn was a big part of what we did out there. But you also have to understand that Shawn's influence begins in the dressing room. He learned the hard way that nothing comes easy and you have to fight and scrap for everything you get on the ice in the NHL. Nothing here is ever easy. He brought that into the dressing room. He really kept the young guys in check and he made sure they didn't take anything for granted. He taught them to respect their elders and to fight for every inch. Then that attitude translated onto the ice.

Every time Shawn went out there, he did everything he could possibly do to help his team win. On a lot of occasions that meant doing the dirty work, and I think that's why among his teammates and around the league, everyone respected him. He was known to be a no-bullshit guy off the ice, and when you put your skates on he was always there to stand up for his teammates.

I think it's important that people understand something else. In 2011, the Bruins would not have won the Stanley Cup without the play of the Merlot Line. Shawn and Soupy (Gregory Campbell) and Piezy (Daniel Paille) had everything—toughness, speed, and skill. They were one of the few fourth lines that could make plays and make a real difference in the game. They took great pride in that. They made the decision easy for Claude Julien to use them against anyone, including the other team's top lines, and that gave our top lines a bit of a break. That played a really, really big role in us winning the Cup that year.

Shawn also had much more skill than people give him credit for. Think about Shawn's penalty-shot goal against Ondrej Pavelec of the Winnipeg Jets. Shawn had never taken a penalty shot, at any level, at any time. I had seen that move from him many, many times in practice, and I knew he had the hands to do something like that. Of course, the surprise was that he actually earned a penalty shot. He had just come out of the penalty box, and there was no other way he was going to get a breakaway!

But he also realized that was his once-in-a-lifetime chance to get a penalty shot in the NHL. The fact that he pulled it off is even more proof that he isn't afraid of anything. I remember he skated toward me, in the goal, and kind of gave me a little bit of a wink, like, *Should I do it?* I kind of knew what he meant, and I said to him, "Hell yes, you should do it!" Then he went down and dangled the goalie out of the net and scored the goal. I was so pumped for him! And I remember everyone else on the bench was so excited for him too.

If you wonder why everyone was so excited, you only have to think about when Shawn took on Matt Cooke after his hit against Marc Savard in 2010. The game is certainly different today, but back then, if you did dirty work on the ice, you had to answer for it. Thorty just never saw it any other way. That was his role over the years, and I knew he couldn't wait to take care of it. For Shawn, it was simple: "You're my brothers, and I look out for you." And he sure did, like so many other times during his career.

Shawn and I actually became boat owners together. Our equipment manager, Keith Robinson, had this boat, and he was looking to sell it. Shawn and I would hang out in the equipment room, and he knew Keito wanted to sell his boat. I lived on a pier in Charlestown, and Shawn also lived in Charlestown, so I said, "Thorty, wouldn't it be great to own a boat, and have it on the dock outside of my place whenever we want to go out?" Shawn was willing, and Keito, being a nice guy, gave us a great price. The next thing I knew, we owned a boat!

I had never owned a boat before, and I'm pretty sure Shawn hadn't either, so now we had this boat sitting on the dock and neither of us had a clue how to use it. Of course, I go to Finland for the summers, so I could almost never use it. When we got it, I had to show Shawn how to operate that boat, and I could barely turn this boat on!

I went home, and Shawn decided he was going to take the boat out to Hull with Erin and another couple. The next thing you know, Shawn bottoms the boat out and takes both engines off. I get a phone call in Finland in mid-July and Thorty says, "I've got a bit of bad news for you. I bottomed the boat out." *Oh, great!*

Look, I only took the boat out two or three times, but I never damaged the boat. But every time he took the boat out, he damaged the boat! At least it was insured, and we got new engines out of it. It was docked outside of my place, and I sat on it many nights having a cocktail, and that was fine by me. What is the old saying—the two best days are the day you buy a boat and the day you sell it?

In all my years with Shawn, I always thought he was going to continue giving back to the game. I know some people don't know this, but he's a very smart guy. He thinks about the game of hockey on a daily basis, including the business side. When he was playing, he would think of the game even from a management side, not just the players' side. He has so much to give. A lot of people who transition from the playing side to coaching look at the game from a certain perspective, but Thorty was always looking at the game from every perspective. He could always think both as a hockey player and as a businessman.

You could see from very early on how involved Shawn was in the community. He always made an impact, from hospital visits to charitable endeavors. That's just how he's built. He wants to meet people and get to know people.

He's one of those characters who are unfortunately dying out in the game today. In these days of social media, guys use that as their way of connecting with people, but Shawn always made a point of getting out there, meeting and connecting with people. Everyone he met felt comfortable around him, and if anyone ever needed anything, Shawn always made sure he was there to help. I think that's why hockey fans in Boston always took to Shawn—he was real.

Shawn is who you think he is. He is real. And he is my friend.

Tuukka Rask is a Vezina Trophy–winning and Stanley Cup–winning goaltender who has played for the Boston Bruins since 2007. He won a bronze medal with Team Finland at the 2014 Sochi Winter Olympics.

PROLOGUE

BOSTON BRUINS FANS WERE PISSED, and I couldn't even blame them. Hell, *we* were pissed. We were pissed at what had happened to our friend and teammate, Marc Savard, and we were pissed at our total lack of response.

Savvy was one of the most talented guys I've ever played with, a player with remarkable skill—a free-agent signing who, along with Zdeno Chara, helped turn around the fortunes of the Boston Bruins. He was a point-a-game guy and helped make us a formidable team to play against. What we didn't know then was that Matt Cooke had, effectively, put an end to a remarkable career. We just didn't know.

It was March 7, 2010, and we were playing the Penguins in Pittsburgh. There was about 5:30 left in the game, and we were down 2–1. Savvy had just released a shot from the high slot toward the Penguins' goal when Cooke caught him in the head, from behind, knocking Savvy out cold. He had to be stretchered off the ice.

This is me talking 10 years later, but I'm not sure it was a completely illegal hit at that point in time in the NHL. It was still a little bit of a gray area. But the lack of a response certainly looks bad. Whoever was behind the play—and I'm *not* trying to throw anyone under the bus here—but I would think your instincts would kick in, and you would try and rectify the situation immediately. But things happen fast! There was a scrum, and you never know. If I was on the ice, something would have happened, but we were also fortunate that we played them not long after that.

I honestly think the guys on the ice didn't realize what had happened. Even on the bench, we were watching the puck after the shot, and didn't really see the hit. We knew Savvy was hurt, but we weren't really sure how or why. But you should know that my instinct is to always defend a teammate, even if the hit is borderline clean.

There was some jawing and jostling, but no real challenge to Cooke, something every guy on the team came to regret almost immediately. We were down a goal late in the third period, and that situation doesn't exactly fit into my skill set, so I never touched the ice again after the hit. I only wish I had.

Look, if anyone hits my teammate, and he's hurt, I'm gonna f—ing kill the guy, or at least try to. Whether it's clean or not, that's just the way I'm wired. But on the other side, Scott Stevens, up until that point, made a living on that exact same thing. And some people say he's the greatest defenseman to ever play in New Jersey. So, if I'm just trying to look at both sides of the spectrum, people in Pittsburgh probably thought it was a clean hit—they had seen Scott Stevens do it for 20 years against them! People in Boston wanted to kill him.

By the time we got to the dressing room we learned how badly Savvy was hurt. We also had a chance to see the video and the hit from Cooke, and everyone on the team was steaming. But by then, there was just nothing we could do.

We caught a fair amount of shit from Bruins fans back in Boston, and I actually understood it. There is a culture in hockey in general, but especially with our team: we are all for one and one for all. You do something to my teammate, you have to pay the price, and Matt Cooke paid no price for his head shot against one of our most skilled players. Sports talk radio was on fire, and we didn't have to listen to WEEI to know what was being said. Fans hated our lack of response, but they didn't hate it as much as we did. Eleven days later, we got to make amends.

We were hosting the Penguins at the Garden on March 18, and emotions were running pretty high. It was our first meeting with Pittsburgh since the Cooke hit, and Savard was still out of the lineup. He would basically miss the rest of the season.

SHANE HNIDY
Bruins teammate

I was in Minnesota when Shawn took on Matt Cooke, and stuck up for Savvy, but I know exactly how it would have gone. Thorty would have told the team, "No one goes near Cooke. Nobody f—ing gets him but me!" That's the type of teammate and type of guy he is. When he has your back, if he says he's going to do something, it's done.

I especially felt that, given my role on the hockey team, this was my responsibility. I had a long talk in the dressing room with our captain, Zdeno Chara, and team leader, Mark Recchi ("Rex"). We knew there were two ways this game could go. The first was a total bloodbath, and we would be all over the *SportsCenter* highlights for the next week, but for all the wrong reasons. Everyone would have to play the game with their head on a swivel, and it was likely that even the game's skill players (like Patrice Bergeron and Sidney Crosby) would not be safe.

The second way the game could go was Matt Cooke had to fight me his first shift of the game. The fight would be fair, and then the matter would be settled. Guys like Patrice and Sid would not have to play the game in fear. The three of us knew how things had to go, but this also involved the cooperation of the Penguins. Or, I should say, it was going to happen with or without their cooperation. We talked about how to connect with the Penguins, and decided Rex would be the guy.

ZDENO CHARA
Bruins teammate, captain

It's not that long ago, but still, it seems like, you know, many, many years more than 10 years ago. Back in those days, those were kind of easy situations to sort out. You would just approach the captain or alternate captain or one of the leaders on the other team, and whether that was the night before or the same day or during the warm-up, nobody cared. But the conversations were pretty clear. Mark Recchi told me and Shawn that he was going to talk to Billy Guerin, because he had known Billy for a long time. I just said, "That's fine, but we've got to respond to what happened to Marc." We stressed that the game could go either way and we gave them the option. Basically, that's what we kind of thought. It was simple. Rex told Billy, "Listen, you know this has to be sorted out. And your guy has to do it even if he doesn't want to. If he doesn't do it, it's gonna be very hard for the skill position players to play this game." Shawn took care of things for us, and to his credit, Matt stepped up too.

PATRICE BERGERON
Bruins teammate

We talked about it before the game. There had been a lot of talk leading up to that rematch, and emotions were running pretty high. We all hated that hit, and we were all wondering what was going to happen. Right after warm-ups Shawn told us in the room, "Hey guys, me and Cooke are going to settle the score, and after that it's over and done with and we play hockey." I thought it was beautifully handled by him and even further proof of his leadership.

We were on the ice at the start of warm-ups, and Rex skated over to stand beside Billy Guerin. Billy is a former Bruin, and an honest and hard-nosed player, but he was playing for the Penguins at the time, and he certainly understood the situation. I have nothing but respect for Billy. Rex told him, in no uncertain terms, that Cooke was going to fight me his first shift of the game, and he was told that if this happened as planned, it was over, no matter what the outcome. I'm told Billy went into his dressing room after warm-ups and told Cooke, in no uncertain terms, what Cooke was going to do.

MARK RECCHI
Bruins teammate

Shawn, Z, and I had a long talk in the dressing room before that second Penguins game, and we were all of the opinion that something needed to be done about Matt Cooke. I knew Billy Guerin, and Billy had been around a long time, so I went to talk to him on the ice at the start of warm-ups. I told him that Matt needed to stand up and answer for what he had done to Marc Savard and Billy just said, "I agree." And he went into their dressing room after warm-ups and told Matt he was going to fight Shawn the first shift.

Shawn really wanted to be the guy to stand up for Savvy, and that's the kind of teammate he was. He looked after his guys all the time. He was a real good player, but obviously he was a very good fighter as well. He felt it was important that he was the guy. I give Cooke a lot of credit too. He stood up.

Shawn has said that if Cooke had not faced him, the game was probably going to be a bloodbath, and that's absolutely what would have happened. The game would have turned pretty ugly. Billy knew that too. He was a smart guy and had been around a long time. He knew things were going to escalate pretty quickly if Matt did not respond.

We were less than two minutes into the game, and I was already near the end of a pretty good shift when Cooke came over the boards. You could wonder about the timing of Cooke's first shift—at the end of my first shift—if you want, but I went straight to him and dropped my stick and gloves. So did he. He had a visor on, and I asked him if he wanted to take the visor off. He said no, so we got to it. I got in a couple of shots, and Cooke went down. I've got to give him credit, because Cooke didn't stop there, and tried to get back to his feet, so I knocked him down again. For the first time in my NHL career, I probably threw a couple of extra punches, but I felt that it was warranted. The Garden crowd was going crazy. They finally felt like I had given them their measure of revenge.

BROOKS ORPIK
Pittsburgh Penguins

We played the night before, and we didn't have a game day skate that day. I was having breakfast and the story in the *Boston Herald* basically said there was a bounty on Cooke for that night. I'm sure that Rexie's story about what was said before the game was right, and I don't have any doubt that Billy Guerin would have relayed that message to Matt.

You've got to tip your cap a bit here. Cooke got back up and played the rest of the game. I was one of the tougher guys in the league at that time—I think I already had more than a dozen fights by that point in the season—and I'm not sure Cooke had that many in his whole career. Look, he got the gloves off, and he stepped up. He can look himself in the mirror, and I can respect that.

We had a bunch of guys who were more than willing to challenge Matt Cooke that night. But I wanted it to be me. Later in the year, after he joined the team, I can remember Gregory Campbell saying, "Shawn, I got this one for ya!" But I knew my role on the team, and I felt it had to be me. We told the coaches before the game that we had already taken care of it, and it was my job to go out and do it. I just told Claude Julien, "Put me out there. Whenever it happens, it happens." I'm not sure Bruins fans would have accepted any other option. It had to be me.

As we were heading toward the penalty boxes—I actually got an additional 10-minute misconduct—I skated directly past a couple of their tougher players (it might have been Eric Godard and Mike Rupp), and I simply asked, "Are we good here?" They both agreed that we were—the matter had been settled properly, and it was over. I think Z fought Mike Rupp later in the game, but that was the only other fight. Guys like Patrice and Sid could play the game the right way. That was part of the thought process. We wanted to go take care of this and then go on with the game and let the players play. I think it was the right way to handle things. We lost 3–0, but this was a game when the score really didn't matter.

I don't like to speak in hypotheticals, but sometimes I wonder what would have happened if Cooke had not accepted the challenge that Bill Guerin gave him. The game certainly would have been a lot more physical, a lot chippier; people would have been getting jumped. I mean, we were in our building and we weren't immune to the negative comments that were being thrown at us.

Matt Cooke played the game a certain way, and I'm sure he felt he had to play on that edge to survive at the NHL level. I also played the game on an edge, but I tried to adhere to a "code" that most guys like me followed. We'll talk more about the code later, but the basics are: don't cheap-shot anyone (and the one time I deviated from the code brings me never-ending regret), don't pick on people smaller than you, always stick up for teammates, and always try to do the right thing.

I couldn't help Savvy and the issues that he was never able to resolve, but I was able to stand up for a teammate and do what I could. I always regret that I couldn't do it at the time of the incident, but I want him to know it mattered to me to stand up for him.

It was one of the times during my career when I tried to do that. But there were many others. So let's get started.

CHAPTER 1

OF JOHN WAYNE AND BOOM BOOM SHAMOON

MAUREEN MILLS IS FROM BELFAST, Northern Ireland. Her husband, Harry, immigrated to Canada in 1960 in pursuit of a better job and a new life. A year later, Maureen and their four daughters followed him to begin their family's new life in Oshawa, Ontario. One of those daughters was Christine, my mom. Maureen and Harry are my grandparents. But, as they say, you may be able to take the girl out of Ireland, but you can't take the Ireland out of the girl.

My Nanny's favorite movie was *The Quiet Man*, a 1952 romantic comedy/drama that earned director John Ford an Academy Award. The movie stars John Wayne as an Irish-born American from Pittsburgh who travels to Ireland to purchase his family's ancestral farm. I'm convinced this movie was her favorite because it was filmed entirely in Ireland (winning another Academy Award for Best Cinematography) and she loved the beautiful Irish countryside.

The John Wayne character is a former prize fighter from the mining area of Pennsylvania who accidentally killed a man in the ring earlier in his career and abandoned the sport forever. The climactic scene in the movie is an epic battle between Wayne's character and a bullying, prosperous landowner named Red Danaher, who also wants to purchase the family farm. Wayne ultimately wins the never-ending fistfight, captures the heart of the beautiful girl (played by Maureen O'Hara), and lives on the farm happily ever after.

The character John Wayne plays in the movie was named Sean Thornton, and my mother named me for my grandmother's favorite character in her favorite movie, although she changed the spelling of the first name. I don't know if I believe in fate or not, but considering my chosen career path, I can't completely discount the possibility that my way in the world was sealed because my grandmother really liked a John Wayne movie.

Like Pittsburgh, Oshawa is a hard-nosed, blue-collar, working man's town. It was made for me—or likely helped make me. My mom, Christine, worked at the Oshawa Hospital as a sterilizing/processing technician, and my dad, Mark, worked in the steel mills—first at Lasco Steel, then at Gerdau Ameristeel. It was hard, back-breaking work, but my father was never afraid of hard work. He's 5'8" and was a steelworker his whole life. Trust me, he's tough. He and my mother instilled that sense of work ethic in both me and my younger sister, Kathleen.

Working in the steel mills is a very tough way to make a living. My dad lost half of his pinkie finger working in those mills. My uncle Bill broke his back in those mills. He basically died, and they had to bring him back to life. I had summer jobs in the mill too, and it didn't take me long to figure out that was *not* the way I wanted to make a living.

My dad worked in steel plants for 35 years, and I don't know how he did it. But it's kind of like that Matt Damon line in the movie *Good Will Hunting*. There's something honorable about showing up and working hard and getting a paycheck, but it's just not how I envisioned my life.

My dad helped me get a summer job at Gerdau, and I had a variety of roles in the steel plant. The manager I was going to be working under was a huge Oshawa Generals fan, but he sort of disliked a certain player. Of course, the steel plant was shift work, and he knew I played hockey outside of the plant with the Peterborough Petes. He mentioned to my dad that if I somehow ended up getting in an altercation with this particular player, and maybe got the better of him, he would try to figure out a way to get me on straight days. Look, the altercation was probably going to happen anyway, but that kind of accelerated the process and I was then able to work straight days, from 7:00 AM until 3:00 PM, Monday through Friday.

That schedule allowed me to work out from 3:30 until 5:30 PM, then go home and try to get something to eat. If I had skating, I would do that at night.

I cut steel bars that came off the cooling bed crooked. They would come off in huge stacks either 30, 60, or 90 feet long. I had a partner at the other end of the bundle, and if a bar was crooked I would rip open the straps, pull out the bad bar, restack the bars, rewrap them, and then cut the defective bars with a torch and toss the pieces back into the recycling plant where they would be melted down again to start over.

I swept the cooling beds. One of the dirtiest jobs I did was during shutdown I had to crawl underneath the area where the steel cooled. Legally, you're only allowed down there for about 15 minutes. I was not claustrophobic, but it was just disgusting down there.

You're lifting steel all day long, so I actually put on weight that summer. When I wasn't working out I was literally lifting steel bars all day. A lot of my muscle development was from my training, but a lot of it was working in that steel plant. I know I was growing out of my shirts pretty quickly that summer.

I had started boxing training with Lionel Ingleton when I was 16, and I knew what a great conditioning workout it is. But I also had an idea that it would help me with what I did on the ice.

I will say that working in the plant was definitely a motivation. But working there also helped instill a work ethic in me. The job I had before that was even worse. I worked straight midnights in a graphic arts factory called Quebecore printing all through high school and one year in juniors, and that was way worse than the plant.

I had seen my dad get in fights—not often, but once in a while—and the rule in our house was, "Don't ever start a fight, but if one happens, don't be afraid to f—n' finish it." I was always told to stick up for other kids—never be a bully, but never get bullied either. My parents are aligned in that. My mom is from Belfast, and Nanny is probably the toughest of all of us. Where I grew up this mattered, because you fought on the playground and you had to stick up for yourself. As long as I didn't start it, I was fine when I came home.

I had a very normal Canadian upbringing in Oshawa, with both parents working and both sets of grandparents around and part of our family. We weren't rich, but we weren't poor, so I can't complain. I made it out of Oshawa without getting into any real trouble, so I guess that's a win.

From a Canadian hockey perspective, I got kind of a late start playing. I didn't play until I was seven and a half, and I don't think I ever had a feeling like, "Hey, I'm pretty good at this!" Truthfully, I was always the worst player on almost every team I was ever on. I guess I just always figured out a way to outsmart, outwork, or outfight enough other guys that I got to stay on the team. I don't think that ever changed.

CHRISTINE THORNTON
Shawn's mom
He was late as far as hockey goes up here. He turned seven in July and started playing hockey that October. I can tell you there was no point during his younger days that I ever thought he was going to be able to make a living playing the game. I'm just being honest. We were absolutely clueless. Shawn was always the last guy to make the team, and I remember him getting cut from a couple of teams.

But there was a moment during my early youth hockey days that helped shape who I became. I was 11 years old and playing in Children's Arena in Oshawa. On the wall in the Arena, they had 8x10 photos of the guys who had made it out of Oshawa. I vividly remember looking at the wall of photos and saying, "Someday, I really want to be up there like those guys." I remember my coach—thankfully I don't even remember his name—telling my 11-year-old self, "Shawn, you're a hard worker, but I don't ever see you being on *that* wall!" And that guy encapsulated my whole career.

I was always the last guy cut or the last guy to make the team. And if I *made* the team, it was, "Well, we better bring in Brian McGrattan because Thornton just might not be that heavyweight that we need." I was just never big enough, never fast enough. And stuff like that *fuels* me! It didn't discourage me, it fueled me. I hope kids reading this who feel like they're on the fringe don't listen to those comments. Just because someone tells you that you can't—don't listen! If you want it bad enough, you can get it.

Doubt me—it just fuels me.

I had to fight, literally and figuratively, my whole life. I've been fighting on the ice since I was 10 or 11 years old. I know how that sounds, but it was different back then. Ten-year-olds certainly don't fight now, and I don't think they should, but back then you had rivalries and you would occasionally have a scrap. You weren't dropping the gloves and ripping each other's faces apart, but we sometimes had fights. I remember a few times we even had parents fighting in the stands.

The only reason I even got a chance to play junior hockey was because of my pugilistic capabilities. I'm not ashamed to say that. I was playing midget hockey in a huge tournament in Quebec, and I was the captain of my team. My goalie got run by this much bigger guy, and I felt it was my duty as captain to do something about it. He was a lot bigger than me, but I ended up kicking the crap out of him pretty bad—mostly because I was scared s—tless and didn't know when to stop.

CHRISTINE THORNTON
Shawn's mom

No, I didn't like to see Shawn play the type of game he did. I'll be honest—there were times when I would just turn my head. I'm his mother, and I certainly didn't want to see him get hurt, especially when he was going up against guys who were a lot bigger. And it seemed like they were all bigger than him!

Peterborough Petes general manager Jeff Twohey happened to be sitting next to my mom, who was talking to the goalie's mom. Jeff said something like, "Who is that kid? Does he fight often?" My mom didn't tell him who she was, or so she told me but she said, "No, he really doesn't fight very often. But I've never seen him lose either." Of course she hadn't been there to see me get my ass kicked in a bunch of playground fights, but that's how I got my tryout with the Peterborough Petes.

JEFF TWOHEY
Former GM, Peterborough Petes

In all my years in hockey—almost 40 years—Shawn is still my favorite scouting story. I was at a tournament in Gatineau, Quebec. It wasn't a very good tournament, but I was there and I had to stay right up until the last game of the day, because that game had two teams I needed to see. But to get to that point I had to sit through a few games that weren't very good, including one with the Oshawa Midgets. Oshawa wasn't very good either, and it was all I could do to stay awake watching this team. They were playing a team from Montreal and Oshawa was getting beat handily. All of the scouts in the building had left before this game, and I was the only guy watching. About halfway through the game, one of the Montreal players ran the Oshawa goalie and then taunted the Oshawa bench. So I

8

watched Shawn grab this kid and beat the crap out of him. His team was down, but he never hesitated and jumped in to defend his team and his teammate. As the fight was unfolding, there was a lady sitting beside me and I could tell she was really into the fight. When it was over, I looked over at her and said something like, "Gee, that kid looks like he knows what he's doing." Now, I don't have anything on identifying who I am, and she looks over and answers, "Well, he's never been beat!" I asked if she knew who the kid was and she just said, "That's my boy!"

Look, I was ready for it, because of my work with Lionel Ingleton. I started working out with him around the age of 16. I would run 12 miles, then we would box and do lunges and stuff. He was really good at getting my mind in a particular space. He would say, "If you're going to make it, you've got to be willing to do things that no one else will do." Lionel was my coach in Atoms and he continued to be a huge factor in my life. He prepared me, physically and mentally, to take my game to the next level. I probably wouldn't have ended up where I did without the input from Lionel.

JEFF TWOHEY
Former GM, Peterborough Petes

I kept Shawn in the back of my mind, and at the end of the season, I used one of my five choices to add him to the OHL draft list. He couldn't be drafted if he wasn't on that list and he had already been through two drafts and never been selected. There was no interest in Shawn Thornton in the OHL. We were sitting at the draft and I told our scouts that this kid was proud. He didn't let an opponent mock his team. There was something there. So we were in the ninth round of the draft, and I stood up and announced that the Peterborough Petes selected Shawn Thornton. I sat down and told the scouts I would contact Shawn after I got home. I didn't get the sentence out of my mouth and suddenly there's a kid standing at our table. I looked at him and asked, "Who are you?" And he just answered, "I'm Shawn Thornton. I was here because my friends were going to get drafted today, and I heard my name." We talked for a couple of minutes and after he got up and left, I turned to our head scout and I said, "Did you see the eyes on that kid? That kid looked right through me, and I've never seen that!"

I went into Petes training camp, and on my first shift they lined me up against a guy named Johnny "Boom Boom" Shamoon. He was the tough guy in Peterborough the year before and I knew exactly what was going to happen. We got the gloves off the first second of my first shift. We squared off and we punched each other in the face for a minute or so. By the end of training camp they decided I was a better hockey player than he was and they kept me around.

DAVE DUERDEN
Petes teammate

Shawn lined up for his first shift of training camp against Johnny "Boom Boom" Shamoon and I think everybody in the city of Peterborough was aware of what was going to happen. I was nervous for Shawn, so I can only imagine what was going through his mind. But I can also tell you it didn't last very long. Shawn earned his way onto that team, and the rest was history.

From day one, I knew that was how I was going to get my foot in the door. Obviously, I worked my ass off, because I don't know any other way, and I tried to become a better hockey player. By my second year, I was playing on the second line and scored 19 goals.

Was I intimidated? No. Was I nervous? Of course I was. It was my first junior camp, and growing up in Oshawa, that's a really big deal.

I was sick to my stomach showing up for my first fitness testing, but I always did what I had to do.

I'm not gonna lie—as a kid growing up in Oshawa, I always dreamed of playing for the Generals, but as soon as I became a Pete that went away. That's when I developed the attitude that I wanted to stick it to the Generals because they didn't want me. Every single time I played against Oshawa I wanted to rub it in their face—every single time.

JEFF TWOHEY
Former GM, Peterborough Petes
Shawn was 18 years old, playing Under-18 hockey on a really bad hockey team. Nobody was watching him, and he had already been cut from basically every Junior B team in the area. I remember talking with some staff from the Oshawa Generals, his hometown team, and when I asked about Shawn they basically just said, "Who is he?" We took a chance on him and gave him an opportunity, and he ended up going to the Memorial Cup final with us. Thorty was a huge part of that. That stuff just doesn't happen in junior hockey, and it's a credit to him because he made the most of the opportunity we gave him.

Our first year in Peterborough we won the OHL title, with Dave MacQueen as the coach. I was a fourth-line guy, and I protected my teammates. I wish I could have contributed more offensively, but I had a role and I played it. I led the Petes with 192 penalty minutes (I think 150 of them were fighting majors), and I knew going into that season what my job was. I was just happy to be there.

It was certainly a different time and place to be playing hockey. There was still hazing, although nothing too egregious. I think I was spared some of it because of who I was and my role within the team. But I remember I had to get up on a table at the high school where I was

11

taking classes with the other first-year guys and sing "I'm a Little Teapot" in front of the whole school. Is that hazing, or is that team building?

I never considered any first-year guy to be a lesser person, but I also felt that a guy who had been in the league for a number of years earned and deserved a certain measure of respect, even if it's little things like getting off the bus first or getting to his room first. To me that's more of a "respect your elders" type of thing.

As captain of the Bruins, Zdeno Chara had a certain leadership style that I respect and honor, but I probably don't feel as strongly about it as he does. He won't even use the term *rookies*, because he feels it gives a sense of lesser worth. But I also feel he should absolutely be the first guy off that bus. He has earned that right.

In my first year of pro hockey with the St. John's Maple Leafs, I had to stop every single day on my way to practice and grab coffee for three of the older guys. I was going to stop and get coffee anyway, so all it cost me was some money from my bank account, but I was happy to do it because it meant that some of these older guys would actually talk to me. I looked at it from the other perspective—it was making me part of the team.

Rookies and young guys pick up the pucks after practice. There is nothing wrong with that. They should be out there for two hours working on their game anyway. In my first five, six, seven years, that's what I was doing. By the time I got to my 18th year, I probably didn't spend as much time out there, but I never thought there was anything wrong with younger guys picking up the pucks. It's not a degrading thing, it's that you haven't earned the right to get off the ice yet. When I was a healthy scratch later in my career, I would still pick up the pucks.

There are certainly areas that are not okay. Even as an 18-year-old kid I didn't have a problem telling guys there were things that just aren't going to happen. If I couldn't look myself in the mirror, or I was putting a teammate in a position where he had a hard time doing that too, then it's just not going to happen. If it was something I was never going to do, why would I ever ask or demand that someone else do it? There has been a lot of news over the past couple of years about junior hockey, and some unbelievably cruel and inhumane instances of hazing and intimidation. None of that is right—never has been and never will be—and I'm happy to see systemic changes in the culture.

I was extremely lucky with my Peterborough experience. It was basically 45 minutes from downtown Oshawa to downtown Peterborough and 35 minutes from my house. My first year, I was living in the basement of my billet family's house—nice people, but the living experience was just different than I was used to.

Then, before my second year, my mom ran into an old friend and co-worker, Janice Boudreau, at a game who asked why she was there. My mom said her son played for the team, and her friend immediately said, "Well, why doesn't he come live with us? We're a big hockey family, and we would love to have him."

That experience was the best. I was like their third child, and the whole family just could not have been better to me. We lived right up the street from the college where I was taking classes.

I had graduated high school before I went to Peterborough. That allowed me a lot of time to focus on hockey. I took a couple of college classes at Sir Sandford Fleming. My plan was to go to college if I didn't get drafted, but I had already graduated from high school so I was able to grab a couple of extra classes for when I had to go to college. I was required to take classes to play in Peterborough, but it wasn't the same as other guys having to take a full-time high-school class load.

My parents would probably tell you I was a smarter kid who didn't apply himself properly in high school. I was a pretty good student—I probably had about a B average—but I didn't put as much effort into it as I should have because I was working toward a goal. I like to think I was smarter than most people expected, given what they thought about what I did. Nothing has ever changed. There is a perception about people who fight, and that's fine. But it's been my goal my entire life to prove people wrong, and I think I'll always feel that way. I felt that way in Peterborough, at every stop in the minor leagues, and everywhere I've played in the NHL.

CHRISTINE THORNTON
Shawn's mom

He was actually a pretty good student and he didn't even try. If he had put any time and effort into it, everyone would have seen how smart he really is. He did well by really doing nothing, which is amazing!

My physical development that summer was probably half because of the steel plant and half because of my training with Lionel Ingleton. His workouts were, shall we say, unique.

Sometimes we would get out on the front lawn with our shoulder pads on, and that's where I started to learn how to grab, where to grab, why not to grab the crux of your opponent's sleeve at the elbow. Sometimes we would put on just one boxing glove and our shoulder pads and go at it. Then we would switch hands. In Sidewalk Square, the first person to bleed or the first person to get knocked out of the square was the loser.

DAVE DUERDEN
Petes teammate

I was one of a bunch of guys who used to go to Lionel's house to train. He had this drill called Sidewalk Square. Two guys would put on the gloves and get into this square on concrete on the sidewalk and try to punch each other out of the square. Lionel had told me that this guy, Shawn, was coming to train with us and he was a pretty tough customer. My first official meeting with Shawn was him punching me in the head—repeatedly. I later learned he was actually taking it pretty easy on me.

Nothing was a better workout for me until later in life, when I discovered jujutsu. It developed my stamina in a way that even skating couldn't. If you watch my fights even later in my career, stamina was never an issue for me. It simply became a question of whether or not I would ever get an opportunity to prove I could play.

CHAPTER 2

TURNING PRO

I WANTED TO PROVE PEOPLE WRONG, but I certainly never thought I was going to get drafted to the NHL. I went to the draft after my first year in Peterborough. It was in St. Louis, and I went there just to meet people. My agent was representing some other guys who were going to get drafted. I was promised a walk-on with Dallas, but that fell through. I ended up getting a walk-on with Colorado and had a decent training camp. I played in an exhibition game and had my first fight in an NHL uniform against Roman Vopat, but I didn't stick. So I was heading back to Peterborough for my second year of juniors. At this point, I'm 19 years old and have basically missed my draft twice.

I remember I was golfing with my buddies Adam Armstrong and Charles Bosworth in summer 1997, and I jokingly said, "Hey, I might have been drafted today!" I was heading back to my house to get a case of beer for the boys after golf when I got a phone call. And on that call I basically told Bill Watters, the assistant general manager of the Toronto Maple Leafs, to f—k off because I thought it was a prank call. He was calling to tell me the Leafs had just drafted me.

It was probably not the best way to begin my pro career, and I think Bill probably still laughs about it, but my foot was in the door. Now it was my job to prove people wrong again. I had to show that I was willing to do whatever it took to make the team and make a difference. It led to a long minor league career and probably a longer NHL career than anyone expected.

I got a letter from the Maple Leafs with all the information about the start of development camp in Toronto, which would begin in the middle of July and run until early August. So we reached out to Bill Watters, and I said, "Look, I'm working in the steel plant and I'm making like $1,000 a week, and my dad had to pull some strings to get me this job. I promise I'll show up in shape, but do you mind if I just show up for training camp in September?"

He gave me permission to miss rookie camp.

I remember getting dropped off at the Holiday Inn by the airport ahead of training camp. I was scared shitless. We had physical testing to start, but it was kind of a blur, partly because I was so afraid. There were guys I knew from junior hockey, and we ended up going out to dinner and getting to know each other. There were a couple of guys at that camp—Brandon Sugden, D.J. Smith, Jeff Ware—who I had actually fought in juniors. If you've fought someone, you actually have a little closer of a bond. I think Smitty and I fought two or three times during training camp and ended up being roommates three of the next four years in St. John's. He's now the head coach of the Ottawa Senators.

DAVE DUERDEN
Petes teammate

We were up in Sudbury, and Shawn had a bout with a kid named Brandon Sugden. Even now, people who don't even know I played will bring up Brandon Sugden's name. He was big (6'4", 235 pounds) and a tough, tough customer. He was one of those guys. It seemed like he would pull a thread or something and all of his equipment would be off. Shawn got off to a pretty good start, and suddenly all of Sugden's stuff is off and he's just out there in a muscle shirt. Shawn had nothing to grab onto, and he was just throwing them. Look, he took some too. But Shawn knew it was one of those make-or-break fights, and it definitely made him.

I just put my head down and went to work every day. I was a little older, and I knew that if I was lucky, I was going to St. John's. I probably migrated toward some of the older guys who had been on that team the year before. I really didn't hang out very much with the Maple Leafs guys during my first training camp.

It was kind of weird for me. Two years earlier, I was in high school and cheering for the Maple Leafs; now I was going out on the ice trying to compete with them. To go on the ice and see Wendel Clark, Tie Domi, and Mats Sundin was kind of daunting. I would think, *All of my friends would pay thousands of dollars just to have a conversation with some of these guys, and now I'm showering with them.* It's something I always tried to remember as my career went forward, and I tried to treat the younger guys who may have been watching me play for a couple of years with respect.

It's kind of hard to explain, but there is something about the culture in hockey. I think it might be the same in rugby. You can be out on the ice, get in a fight, and just kick the crap out of each other, but you're just as likely to grab a beer with the same guy that night. Smitty and I still go back and forth about who was tougher—blah, blah, blah. Normally there are no hard feelings; it's just part of the job. You respect the other person for having to do it as well.

I'll give you an example. After one game, I ended up in the same after-hours establishment as Jody Shelley. We had fought earlier in the evening and happened to run into each other at, like, three in the morning. It quickly became, "Oh, hey man, how are ya?" We sat down, had a beer, and actually got to know each other a little. Then we fought again something like seven times after that. It's just part of the job.

21

That sort of thing actually happened a bunch. St. John's was a little different too. Most of the teams stayed over after the game. It was kind of like Halifax, but on a smaller scale. There were only a few bars that you would go to. There are about 30 of them on a quarter-mile strip, but there are nights aligned with particular spots. Friday night was Turkey Joe's. Saturday night was Green Sleeves. Teams stay over and you'd run into them at the same places. There were a lot of tough guys playing in the league at the time. Chances were, you were going to be drinking with them. As long as it didn't get out of control, you would usually have a beer with a guy.

When I was in Leafs camp, the player who probably caused me to go, "Holy s—t! That's ____!" was Wendel Clark. I've gotten to know him over the years now and played some golf with him, and he's just a great guy! But he was an icon in Toronto. He was the captain of the Maple Leafs, he scored 40 to 50 goals, and he was only 5'10" but was fighting Bob Probert and all of the big boys. He was the Cam Neely of Toronto, but a lot smaller. Not taking *anything* away from Cam, but Cam was surrounded by tougher guys than Wendel was, so Wendel was probably having to fight tougher guys too.

The very first time I saw Wendel it was truly a *holy s—t* moment! First off, I was a little bit bigger than him, and I'm not sure if he could kick my ass, but I know he had no problem f—ing trying! And I had watched him through my whole adolescent years. He was the guy who was just different for me.

Training camp was also just different for me, and was certainly not like it was when I went to Peterborough. I only fought a couple of times. I fought this poor kid named Marek Posmyk from the Czech Republic. He was 6'5" or 6'6". He was running around and hitting people—just trying to play a hard game. By that time, veteran NHL enforcer Greg Smyth was playing for St. John's, and he said, "Who the f—k is this guy!" So I just went out there and grabbed him because I wanted to impress the older guy, the super vet on the team, and I thought it was the right thing to do. I think I broke Posmyk's nose. There was a picture on the front page of the sports section in one of the Toronto papers and he was just laid out on his stomach, holding his nose. I kind of felt bad. But Bird Dog had basically said, "Who is going to take care of this?" and I thought, "I'm going to have to do this for the next three years, so I better let them know who I am right now." And Bird Dog loved it!

My only focus in that first training camp was making the American Hockey League team. I just didn't want to get sent back to juniors as an overage player or to the East Coast Hockey League team—I think it was in Pensacola at the time. Not too many guys who went there got called back up. Geographically and psychologically, it was a *long* way away!

We were in the off-season after my second year in St. John's when Tie Domi called me and asked what I was doing. He told me I had 15 minutes to get to his place. I hustled over, and Tie took me out to a wonderful dinner in Toronto. After dinner, we might have also gone out for a drink or two. At the end of the evening, I was going back to my friend Hubie Hutton's apartment, where I was living that summer, and Tie was heading back to his place in the city when he pulled me close.

Tie gave me a hug and stuck his hand into my pocket. He told me to not say a word and just accept what he was giving. When I got back to Hubie's place, I pulled $2,000 out of my pocket. I called Tie, and he told me this was something Mark Messier had done for him, and he was paying it forward. He told me that he knew there was uncertainty about where or if I would play at all, and that I should take the money and pay my bills and make sure I was okay to start the season, wherever I was playing. I can't tell you what that meant to me. He just told me when I made the NHL I could pay him back.

A number of years later, I was coming out of the Bruins dressing room and Tie was outside talking with Cam Neely. I told him to stay right there, and I ran back into my locker stall and grabbed my checkbook. I wrote a check for $2,000 and went back to the hall to give it to Tie. He never expected to get it back, but it meant a lot to me to be able to repay him. It took me 10 years to make it full-time, but I got to pay it back.

Back to training camp. We had this eight-game exhibition series sponsored by Molson Canadian that was basically St. John's against Fredericton. I'll come back to this series later, but I believe I had 128 penalty minutes in eight games, and I was three fights and out a couple of times. I fought every single night and was getting acupuncture in my hands before games and icing them down. I was actually suspended for my first game in the AHL because I got suspended in my last exhibition game for head-butting someone.

I never even got an exhibition game with the Leafs until my third year of professional hockey. My second year in the AHL I was second in the league in penalty minutes, I think to Aaron Downey, and second in fighting majors, with 36. I went into training camp feeling pretty good about myself. I had fought anybody and everybody, but Toronto still had Tie Domi, Wade Belak, Kris King, and a bunch of other tough guys, so I knew I wouldn't be on the roster.

I remember I had a great conversation with Pat Quinn. They were sending me down and I had my interview with Pat, and he said, "You might be the toughest guy I've ever seen. You might be the toughest guy in the AHL, and you might be the toughest guy here, but I still wouldn't have you on my team. You can't play a lick!"

I thought I was a decent hockey player, but when Pat told me that I thought, *Holy s—t!* St. John's head coach Al MacAdam was in the room at the time, and I thought he might add something positive to what Pat had said, but nothing. It sunk in. I took it to heart. I wasn't offended by it. I didn't walk out pissed. I mean, this is Pat Quinn, who is really tough, but I need to get to work on being a better hockey player. I didn't know Pat all that well, but I admired the man.

My first year in St. John's we weren't very good. It was a tough league, and we had a young team. Toronto had a bunch of draft picks, but we just weren't that good. Looking back, we didn't really have any top-end, grade A prospects down there, myself included. Greg Smyth made it for a while, and maybe me, D.J. Smith, and Kevyn Adams, but not too many guys from that roster made a mark in the NHL. Mark Deyell was actually racking up points and was looking pretty good, but he ended up losing his eye. We weren't very good, but we were a pretty tough team. I do know that.

You make the move from juniors, where you're fighting kids your age, to the pros, and suddenly you're fighting grown-ass men. It took me a full year to get my legs underneath me. It really wasn't until my second year that I felt comfortable doing it.

But I *loved* St. John's. It's winter from the time you get there until the day you leave, but it's full of just great, great people—actually the *best* people. It's the people who make that place. I had about 100 people at my wedding, and probably 30 of them were Newfies. I think I still keep in touch with like half of those people. Two or three of my best friends in the world are Newfies from my time out there.

I probably didn't think it was going to take as long as it did to get to the NHL. My first year in St. John's I was just happy to be there. My mind didn't shift until I got to Chicago and saw guys like Aaron Downey and Ryan VandenBussche actually playing in the NHL. I thought, *Well, f—k, I played against these guys and I actually think I'm maybe a better player than both of them, and equally as tough.* So I thought, *If they can do it, then I can do it.*

I'm coming up through Toronto's system, and I'm seeing Tie Domi, Kris King—guys I grew up watching. And I'm thinking, *Well, I'm not* those *guys, so I'm good down here in the American League.* At least I'm next in line if maybe something happens. But then I got to Chicago and its minor league team in Norfolk, Virginia, and saw some of the players on other teams. I see Jody Shelley in Columbus and I'm thinking, *I played way more minutes and a bigger role in the minors.* I thought I was a better player, and we fought, so I felt I was just as tough as him. That's when my eyes were opened. I realized I probably needed a fresh start and I also needed to reassess my life a little bit. I needed to get a little more serious about the training and the dedication I needed to get to the next level.

The year before, we'd had Clayton Norris and a couple of other older guys who helped out, but my second year in the AHL there were a bunch of younger guys who were in my weight division, and I just thought that if I was going to do this, I had to hold my own against them. Guys like Rocky Thompson, Aaron Downey—all these kids who came out of juniors and were starting to fight all the big boys and lead the league in penalty minutes. I thought, *Well, they're doing it, and if I want to get noticed then I'm gonna have to do it too.* I put it on my shoulders—and I did it.

ERIN THORNTON
Shawn's wife

He had been playing in the minors for quite a while and was beginning to think he wasn't going to be able to make the jump to the NHL. So I had a talk with him, and said, "If this is really what you want to do with your life, then maybe you need to tailor a few things differently." He worked hard, but he ate like crap; he went out at night and drank his face off. I just told him he couldn't continue to live like that and get to his ultimate goal. So I helped him change his diet and schedule, but I didn't want to have anything to do with his training, especially on the ice. When he got to training camp he had one of the best body fat and testing scores that year. He always had that within him, he just had to stop being a kid and start being a professional.

My second year in the AHL, I played 78 games and had 36 fights. That's almost one every other night. Sometimes it was two in a game and there were probably a few with three in a game. But I was basically doing it every other night, and a lot of the guys were bigger than me. My hands were a mess. There were some nights that I couldn't hang onto my stick because my forearms were so tight with tennis elbow from gripping jerseys. I was fighting and trying to play hockey, playing defense a majority of the time and forward some of the time. But that was the league back then. There were five or six guys like that on every single team!

We went into Saint John, New Brunswick, and they had Rocky Thompson, Matt Audette, Chris Dingman, Eric Landry, Steve Begin. I had to fight every night. You just do it.

If I took Pat Quinn's comments to heart, that meant I also had to work on my game. Rich Brown, the assistant coach, used to grab me every day after practice. If there was a two-hour practice allotment, I didn't leave the ice until the two hours were over. It didn't matter if I was out with the boys; you still have to get up with the men. I had to get in and ride the bike, get on the ice, and put my work in, and that meant staying on the ice for the full two hours. I would be stick-handling between pucks, shooting pucks on empty nets or the backup goalie, three-on-three in one zone. Every single day I was working on something to make myself better. But I also had coaches who would stay out there and work with me for the whole two hours. I'm not sure how common that is these days.

I actually worked my way up to playing the back end on the power play my second year. Al MacAdam liked me and thought I had good poise with the puck. I played defense most of the year, either paired with Bird Dog or D.J. Smith, so I got a good amount of ice time. My first year, I was the grocery stick. We played three lines plus one and six defensemen, so if a defenseman went down I would play defense. If a forward went down I would play up front. Some nights I just sat in the middle of the bench and didn't do a damn thing except chirp the other team and cheer on my teammates.

TERRAN SANDWITH
St. John's teammate

Back in the AHL days, Shawn was a little bit of a showboat. He had a little bit of the WWE in him. He would play it up for the crowd, and he was a little bit ridiculous. Of course, Shawn was our heavyweight, but we had three or four guys who were right there with him. He really wasn't a heavyweight but he would fight guys who *were* heavyweights. He was just *not* going to get beat. I played with a lot of tough guys, but I've got to say his mentality for fighting was second to none. And Shawn isn't a meathead. He tended to play with a bit of a screw loose on the ice, but he wasn't like that off the ice.

I caught mono in my third year, and it cost me pretty much the last month of the season. We didn't make the playoffs; I think I was at the Kentucky Derby that year. Bird Dog had moved on from player to an assistant coach by my third year, but he got fired about halfway through the season for an altercation with some of my teammates. He was a great teammate, but one of the craziest people I've ever met. A real trigger was if someone called him dumb, and let's just say that during a long night in Portland, Maine, he and I ran into a couple of teammates who made that mistake. There might have been a chase down the street involved too. I honestly didn't think the big man could move that fast. The next day at practice Al said to me, "Yeah—no more Bird Dog."

In all, I played four seasons in St. John's—and loved every minute of it. The Maple Leafs didn't qualify me by a certain date, and I was told they no longer owned my rights. The Players Association told me I could go shop myself around and the Leafs told me they weren't signing me. I guess they didn't want me around anymore.

I didn't have an agent at the time, so I called every single general manager in the NHL myself; then I called every single assistant GM and coach in the minors. I had some good talks with different teams. Al MacIsaac, who was with the Norfolk Admirals, the Chicago Blackhawks' minor league affiliate at the time, said they would love to have me. Mike Smith, who was in Toronto for part of my time there, was in Chicago by then, so the Blackhawks gave me a tryout and an AHL contract. I signed the deal, went to camp with the Blackhawks, and, at the end of camp, Smith called and said they wanted to sign me to an NHL contract. He asked who my agent was. I said, "Me." He said, "Well, I'm going to give you an extra $5,000 to play in the minors for not having to deal with an agent!"

I don't know if I ever had an idol growing up watching hockey, but if I did, Bob Probert was probably it. For Christmas every year, my grandmother would get me the Don Cherry "Rock 'Em, Sock 'Em" videos and we would sit in my living room watching them. I might have watched them more than everyone else. Don Cherry loved Bob Probert, and Bob was probably everything I ever hoped to be as a hockey player.

So I'm in my first training camp with the Chicago Blackhawks and I report to the hotel. The young lady behind the desk tells me, "Oh, you're rooming with Mr. Probert." *Holy shit!*

I go to the room, and later that evening, when the veteran Blackhawks players have to show up, the door opens and there is Probert. He's carrying his suitcase and a bag from P.F. Chang's. The first words ever from Bob Probert to me were, "Hey...you want some lettuce wraps?"

Bob was kind of winding down his playing career at that point and would ultimately work his way into the broadcast booth. But I was one of the guys who could potentially replace him, and I wondered how he would look at that. There were times when I was heading into practice and thought about the possibility that Bob Probert would want to protect his territory and tune me up. But he never did.

Bob couldn't have treated me better and couldn't have been more supportive. He was everything I ever hoped one of my primary hockey influences could be and more. We had a tough team, with guys like Chris Simon, Lyle Odelein, Louie DeBrusk, and Ryan VandenBussche, but no one was tougher than Bob Probert and no one was more supportive than him. I loved that guy.

I signed a two-year deal with the Norfolk Admirals and the Maple Leafs put in a claim, saying they still owned my rights. The union evidently didn't stick up for me because I wasn't a big enough deal to set a precedent with. So I had been to camp, had been sent down, and I was in Norfolk at Marty Wilford's house. His wife had made dinner for us. The phone rang, and Marty was told he had just been traded—for me—while I was sitting in his house. I guess Chicago had a list of players it was willing to part with in exchange for me, and Marty's name was on the list.

Marty's wife, Shelly, was a videographer for one of the TV stations and had a good job in Virginia Beach. There were no cell phones back then, so the call came to Marty's house and he was told he had been traded for the guy sitting in his living room. I was staring at him as he picked up the phone in his kitchen and told Shelley they had just been traded to St. John's, Newfoundland. Shelly was from Iowa, and she said, "Where the f—k is that? And who did you get traded for?"

He ended up re-signing with Norfolk the following year, and I played with him for a couple of years. But the amount of hugs I had to give Shelly to apologize for being shipped to St. John's was unbelievable. I wish I could make this s—t up, but this is my life!

I had come from four years in St. John's, where the snow came up to the roof. D.J. Smith, Donald MacLean, and I lived in a house by the airport, and we would open the sliding door in the back of the house and jam beers in the snow. Our back door was our beer fridge after the games.

We went on a two-week road trip and we had so much snow that my car got buried, and we didn't dig it out until May. From February until May we couldn't find my car because it was buried in snow. I went from that to living the beach life. It was a culture shock, but it was a breath of fresh air, that's for sure.

CHAPTER 3

BIRD DOG AND THE ROCK

I'VE GOTTA BE HONEST WITH YOU. When the Toronto Maple Leafs sent me down to St. John's, Newfoundland, I had *no* idea where it even really was. I had to do a little research and look on a map, but even that didn't do it justice.

I got off the plane after being sent down and I hopped in a cab, heading for the Holiday Inn, which was the team hotel. The cab driver started grilling me with a *very* thick Newfoundland accent. "Where are you from, where are you staying, what are you doing for dinner?" I'm thinking to myself, *Wow, is this guy friendly!*

I told him I was in town to try out for the Baby Leafs, I was heading to the Holiday Inn, and I just planned on having dinner at the hotel. He was having none of that. "Oh, no. Your first night in Newfoundland you can't be eating in a hotel. I'm gonna get the misses to cook you up a jig!" Now I'm thinking, *What the hell is going on here? This is my cab driver and he just invited me over for dinner? He's never met me, I'm from Toronto, and I'm probably going to be chopped into little pieces and buried in his basement.*

Now, I didn't go have dinner cooked by the missus. I just ate at the hotel like I had planned. But after living on the Rock for four years, I came to learn that it was a genuine invitation. The culture there, where residents greet people with an open heart, reminds me a bit of

Ireland. That cab driver was very sincere that I should not have to eat in a hotel my first night in the province. In his mind, that's not what Newfoundland was about. I should come home with him and become part of the family for the night.

In my four years in St. John's, it was winter from the time I arrived until the time I went home. But the people were some of the greatest human beings I've ever met in my whole life. I always felt that Oshawa was a very friendly town too, but the people in Newfoundland were a whole other world.

It would be easy to think the down-to-earth people of St. John's would take to the type of player I was, but our team was so tough that we had about eight different heavyweights for all four years. It certainly wasn't just me. It was everyone. It felt like the whole island just got along.

We would go down to Green Sleeves for dinner and the owner would come out, sit down, and have dinner with us. It certainly wasn't warm temperature-wise, but it was such a warm and welcoming place to live and work.

On 9/11, not long after the second plane hit the World Trade Center, air travel was suspended across America, and a lot of planes en route from Europe had to find someplace else to land. Well, 38 of those planes were forced to land in Gander, Newfoundland, and that meant almost 6,700 people needed a place to stay. The people of Gander took the passengers into their homes, their schools, and anyplace else they needed to shelter and take care of them.

Gander opened up its stores and gave away products for free just to help. Residents took people they didn't know into their homes and gave them food, shelter, safety. Those 6,700 passengers doubled the population of Gander, and the people who lived there didn't care a bit. That is what St. John's and all of Newfoundland was like.

We all were trying like hell to make it to the National Hockey League, and we were willing to do anything to get there. But we always joked in St. John's that we were treated like the Toronto Maple Leafs, but in a much smaller town. They loved hockey, and they loved the team, and we were part of their community. Any of us who played there still has a lot of lifetime friends who are from there or still live there. I have really fond memories of my time there.

My wife and I became engaged driving back there one summer just to visit people. We spent two weeks there a couple of years after I had left St. John's. We were staying at The Delta, which is a hotel downtown, and we went to Green Sleeves for dinner. The owner, Dick Hancock, was so happy to see me and so happy to meet my new fiancée, Erin. When he asked where we were staying, I told him The Delta, and he got mad at me!

"Don't you ever stay at The Delta again! I'll move out of my house and you can both stay at my house as long as you need to before you ever stay at a hotel again." And he was serious. It wasn't just words. He would have moved into a hotel, and we would have been sleeping in his house.

When I got there, I did everything I had to do to make the team, and I did. I dressed in almost 60 games, and I probably played in about 48.

I first met Greg Smyth in training camp, because I knocked out Marek Posmyk in that camp fight. Then I got sent down to St. John's and really got to know him. He was the "uber vet" on the team. He was really good about taking care of the young guys on the team, and that's what I was that first year. And because I also fought, he kind of took a liking to me.

There were four seats in the back of the bus with a card table built in. The two veteran guys on the team would have those four seats to themselves. Greg's nickname was Bird Dog, so those four seats became the "Bird Bath." I was one of the only guys on the team who was allowed to go sit in the Bird Bath and have beers with them. I was fighting 25 or 30 times a year, so I guess that got me a little extra consideration. He took care of me.

Bird Dog wasn't just tough. I saw him lose his share of fights, just like the rest of us. But he was legitimately *crazy*, in the best kind of way. My second year in St. John's, Bird Dog played in 40 games, and he was suspended for the other 40. But he taught me some valuable lessons back in that first year too.

He would say, "Thorty, if you go into a pile, you go in with all guns blazing. You have your gloves off and you grab somebody. If they look at you even slightly off, then you just start throwing. If you don't, they're going to."

He also said, "You're 6'1", 200 pounds, so you're gonna have to do something every once in a while just to make them think you're crazy, even though you're not." He told me there were going to be games when I might have to cross-check somebody in the face—if they deserve it. But that was just so I didn't have to fight every single night. In that league, at that time, I would have had to fight every single night if people weren't afraid of me.

But Bird Dog also held me accountable. He would be as hard on me as anyone, then he would invite me to the Bird Bath after the game. We would have a beer, then the next day he would be slashing me in the shins if I tried to go around him in practice if I wasn't competing. Or he would slash me in the back of the legs and try to get me to fight him in practice. But if I ever got in trouble, he would have been the first person I would call because I knew he would have given me the shirt off his back.

We were at practice one day, and Bird Dog was chirping D.J. Smith about how bad his shot was. So they made a bet. D.J was at the blue line, and Bird Dog went into the net wearing his regular equipment and blocked slap shots from Smitty for twenty bucks because he just wanted to chirp him about how bad he shot the puck. Smitty had to score eight of 10 to win his bet, and I think Bird Dog gave up one.

We were playing Fredericton in the playoffs one year, and during the morning skate, I was sitting in the stall next to Bird Dog. We had a certain practice time lined up after Fredericton finished up with its skate. All of a sudden, Bird Dog just started yelling, "They're f—ing with us! They're just f—ing with us!" He thought they were taking too long, and that we were supposed to be on the ice by that time.

So he went out to the ice, half-dressed—no shoulder pads or elbow pads—grabbed his stick, stepped on the ice, and just started firing slap shots at their taxi squad that was getting a skate in after their team practice. Bird Dog didn't tell anyone he was doing this; he just headed out there. He cleared the ice, *by himself*, firing slap shots at all of them. He was shooting at their goalie coach and anyone else who was out there. Their tough guy, Dave "Moose" Morissette, came out of their dressing room, and Bird Dog started firing pucks over the boards *at* Morissette! So he cleared the ice and came back into the dressing room, grabbed his coffee, and calmly said, "Zamboni should be on any minute now, boys."

Bird Dog got suspended for 15 games one time for something that happened in Portland. Portland was up by four or five goals, and a kid named J.P. Dumont lightly brushed Bird Dog, just finishing his check in the corner with about 2:00 left in the game. Bird Dog skated out to the blue line, cross-checked Dumont in the face as hard as he could, knocked him to his knees, then cross-checked him in the back of the head.

D.J. Smith went to talk to the referee, and the ref put his hand up and said, "Don't even try! I don't want to hear it!" And D.J. said, "No, no! I just want to know what jail we need to pick him up at!"

Bird Dog's first game back from the suspension was in Hamilton. Danny Lacroix ran our guy, Aaron Brand, from behind really bad. I was on the ice and I jumped Lacroix and fought him immediately. There was a 5-on-5 line brawl, and Lacroix got kicked out of the game. Lacroix started to head down the tunnel, and out of the corner of my eye I saw Bird Dog leave the bench and head down our tunnel.

I skated off the ice and sprinted down the tunnel trying to catch Bird Dog. On his way, Bird Dog grabbed about five sticks, but tossed all but

39

one of them on the ground. He walked over to where Lacroix would have been coming down the tunnel. He took a full baseball swing at the tunnel opening, and thank God Danny Lacroix saw him coming and fell backward on his ass, or Bird Dog might have killed him. The stick shattered against the cement wall. Security grabbed Bird Dog and got a chain link fence into place that was supposed to separate the dressing rooms. Bird Dog grabbed the sticks and was jumping and throwing them like spears into the crowd of people that had gathered. He was vowing to kill the man, so he got another 12-game suspension for that one. That wasn't Bird Dog "acting" crazy, that was him *losing his mind* because someone had taken advantage of his teammate.

Let's make one thing clear. I had enough maturity to understand what should and shouldn't be allowed, so for that reason Bird Dog was a *great* influence on me. I was never wired to do the things he did, and he definitely went way over the line. He was 33 when I was 20, so he came from a different time...a time when bench-clearing brawls happened twice a game. Off the ice, he couldn't have been a better human being.

AL MacADAM
Head coach, St. John's Maple Leafs

I loved Greg Smyth. He was just like Shawn in his passion and he was the last of a dying breed as far as the game was concerned. He was certainly more helpful to Shawn than not. Shawn would step onto the ice from day one with a pro attitude, ready to work. Greg, no matter what he did the night before, would show up early, and *he* came to work. But if you remember Danny Markov, Greg took *him* under his wing as well, and you could see the upside and the downside of his being a mentor. But deep down, Shawn had the right stuff.

Bird Dog was from Toronto, but when he retired, he moved back to Newfoundland and spent the rest of his days there. He fully embraced the culture. He was a Newfie through and through even though he was born in Toronto.

He was one of the biggest influences for 20-year-old athletes like me to get out of our shells and be a part of the community. He always said we were no better than anyone else who lived in St. John's and we needed to embrace the people the way they embraced us. He was an OHL All-Star and a second-round pick, but he was also a man of the people. He was a great influence on me in that regard.

We would occasionally have bench-clearing brawls, although line brawls were much more common. To be honest, I started a line brawl one time against Fredericton. I jumped off the bench, so I guess technically it was a 6-on-5 brawl, and I was the sixth guy. We thought everything through. We had tie-downs back then, but we would also wear goalie-cut sweaters, and the sleeves were a lot bigger so you could get out of them quicker.

You'll hear much more about an eight-game exhibition series across the Maritimes later on, but this is a story about one of those games. We were in Grand Falls, and after the game, we all went to the hotel bar to have a few beers. There were a bunch of locals there. We were a bunch of young hockey players, and obviously *not* local. We were having a few beers and having a good time, but no one was antagonistic. And let me emphasize—Bird Dog was *not* there! He was actually very angry that he wasn't.

I was standing at the bar with Danny Markov, and Danny didn't speak English very well. Somebody was trying to talk to him, and he wasn't responding, so somebody threw a punch. So Markov responded with, "F—k you very much!" Then a total bar brawl broke out. It was us against the bar. It was out of a movie. At some point I was fighting two guys, and D.J. Smith was fighting a couple of guys. We ended up getting escorted out of the bar.

The next day, I had scratches all over my face and other guys had black eyes. Somebody had cover-up in their bag, and we were trying to hide the damage from the night before. And I remember Al MacAdam saying to us at practice, in his Al MacAdam way, "Sometimes when the bear is poked, you need to stand up to the bear. Sometimes, it's better to walk away from the bear. Last night, you guys decided to fight with the bear. Next time, I would appreciate it if you would walk away from the bear."

It's fair to say no one on either side was going to be pressing charges. But as I said, on the ice, I was fighting every single night. So part of me was thinking fighting was the last thing I needed to be doing after a game, but the other part was thinking, *This is a teammate and he needs help.* This wasn't a hockey fight. Your primal instincts kick in and you make sure you do whatever it takes to get out of there in one piece. In hockey fighting, you're thinking about it all day, and you're building up to it. With this, it was quick and we didn't have time to think.

Bar challenges didn't really happen with me very much. I really am the quiet guy who just sits in the bar and enjoys his beer and doesn't want anything bad to happen. I'm very friendly with everyone and I truly don't have an antagonistic bone in my body. Erin will tell you that I avoid conflict at all costs outside the game of hockey.

I've had people joke about testing me. Once or twice, I've had people try to start things with friends of mine. I usually walk over and tell those types, "You know who I am, right? You think I'm tough? Well, these two guys would kill me, so just keep that in mind." That squashed the situation one time. The only times I ever fought off the ice were when my friends were in a fight and I had to get involved—when I was much, much younger!

I'm not sure my game developed at the pace I might have wanted in St. John's. I was a little insecure about the guys I was fighting, the timing, and how often I was doing it. I was unsure of myself, so I would try to make up for that. I was also immature and guilty of too many antics, going over the top with barking and screaming and yelling. I was a lot more concerned about fighting than I was about playing.

Back then I just thought if I beat up everybody in the AHL and fought 35 or 40 times a year, someone in the NHL would notice and give me a job. While that sort of thing was happening for a bunch of guys at that time, it didn't happen for me. I was so lucky that Al MacAdam put a lot of trust in me and showed confidence in my game. I played defense a lot more my first two and a half seasons up there. Our assistant coach, Rich Brown, put a lot of time and effort into helping me get better. We would stay on the ice for as much as two hours after practice working on stick-handling, shooting drills, and skating.

I remember when I got to Norfolk and my coach, Trent Yawney, said, "Thorty, the fighting will take care of itself. I need you to focus on playing the game. You're tough enough. Stop worrying about it. No one is going to beat you up in this league. You've already proven it—you've beaten everyone else up!" That was a wake-up call, like the one from Pat Quinn, to work on my game. It helped me.

I wish I could tell you we were more successful in St. John's, but we didn't have very good teams. I don't think we got out of the first round. Those were kind of the glory years in Toronto with guys like Mats Sundin and Curtis Joseph, but that didn't trickle down to our minor league team.

I'm not gonna lie—when I went to Norfolk I really missed St. John's. I kind of felt like I had been pushed out by Lou Crawford, and it bothered me. I guess if I wasn't going to get a chance in Toronto, it was time to move on, but I also didn't think the move to Norfolk was going to get me any closer to the NHL at the time. It worked out the opposite of what I had thought, but I didn't know that at the time.

The Chicago team I was signing on with had guys like Chris Simon, Aaron Downey, Ryan VandenBussche, and Bob Probert, so they didn't need a player like me at the NHL level. They were just signing me for their minor league team in Norfolk. Then a year or so later, some of those guys moved on, and I suddenly had an opportunity that I didn't anticipate.

CHAPTER 4

FROM WINTER TO SUMMER

AFTER FOUR YEARS IN ST. JOHN'S where it was never *not* winter, going to Norfolk was a nice little change. It was an adjustment for sure. I didn't know anybody on the team, but they turned out to be a great bunch of guys. My first year in Norfolk I ended up living with a guy named Matt Henderson, a kid from Minnesota, and we got along really well. We had a really tight team. We lived midway between Norfolk and Virginia Beach. It was the best of both worlds.

By my second year in Norfolk, Erin was with me, and she got a bit of a wake-up call about what life was like in the minors. I had started that season in Chicago, but when I got sent down Erin got to see that life in the AHL was a completely different animal.

Some guys rented some big houses and lived together, but a bunch of us lived in one big building at The Edgewater. We lived right on the beach. There were a bunch of families living in the same complex. Quentin Lang and his wife were there, and we were very close with them. We were also close with Jason Morgan, and he ended up living with us for a while.

ERIN THORNTON
Shawn's wife
We all lived at 3615 Atlantic Avenue in Virginia Beach. Basically the entire team lived in the same building. It was like *Upstairs, Downstairs*. We would all be doing crockpot dinners before we left for the game, then the guys would come home after the games and we would travel to each other's houses and have dinner together. It was very tight-knit, and Shawn and I loved it.

Louie DeBrusk and his wife, Cindy, were there, which meant a very young Jake DeBrusk was there as well. I played with Louie all year. When Jake got drafted by the Bruins in 2015, I was watching in my kitchen in Charlestown, and it was one of the few times I remember the hair standing up on the back of my neck. I remembered him as a six-year-old kid coming on some of the long road trips on the bus with us. That's probably when I knew it was time to retire.

I was 26 years old at the time and Louie helped me out a lot. Louie didn't play a lot of games that year and ended up becoming kind of a de facto player-coach. Louie and I became pretty tight. I would say I had some anger management issues at the time and I was still very emotional. Our coach, Trent Yawney, would hold me accountable. I didn't always understand why, and Louie did a good job of helping me get what I was being told. He also did a good job of explaining to Yawns how I was wired and how I got myself ready to do the job I had to do, even if I wasn't always comfortable doing it. Sort of like Louie was. He helped so much with that relationship, even if he didn't know how much he meant to me.

Louie was a different kind of mentor than Greg Smyth was— certainly a little more level-headed. But Louie had already played 400 games in the NHL by that point, so he was at a different point in his career. He was like me off the ice—really happy, mild-mannered. Bird Dog was *not* mild-mannered! Louie was mostly a friend, but he was a mentor as well.

LOUIE DeBRUSK
Teammate, Norfolk Admirals

We would ride to games together and I remember getting four or five espresso shots on our way to the rink. People don't understand, but you have to get yourself to a place most people just can't get to. When you play the way we did, you have to be a bit selfish in your preparation. Tough guys and goalies are the only two positions that almost have to speak a different language than the rest of the team. I know this about Shawn Thornton—I couldn't have done what he did. He always fought bigger guys, but he was a good technical fighter and he had *big balls*! He had to fight for every g–d d—n inch.

Trent Yawney was a different coach from Al MacAdam and a different coach from Lou Crawford. Trent was new-school in some ways and very old-school in others. He was perfect for me at the time.

It's not like I had to completely reestablish myself when I went to Norfolk. I had already played four years in St. John's, and four years in the minors is a fairly long time. I was going into my fifth season, so at that point you're usually either on to the NHL or you've established yourself at the AHL level. I was young in "real" life, but in the minors I had a few years on the other guys.

There were some nights when the game felt a little more laid-back in Norfolk than it was in St. John's. I was maturing a little, although I was still fighting a ton. I was averaging close to 300 penalty minutes. But Yawns had told me to focus on playing and that the fighting would take care of itself. He told me that everyone already knew how tough I was.

TRENT YAWNEY

Head coach, Norfolk Admirals and Chicago Blackhawks

I didn't know much about Thorty when he came to Norfolk, other than that he was tough and had fought every tough guy in the American Hockey League. In one of his first games after we traded for him he just beat the s—t out of some guy. After the fight there were all these theatrics and he was spinning his helmet as he went to the penalty box, and I'm thinking, *Oh boy! This has got to stop!* So I had a talk with him, and I told him I didn't like him bringing all that attention on himself. Everyone already knew he was tough. So I made a pact with him. I knew he was going to fight from time to time, but if he stopped all the theatrics after the fight I would get him more ice time on the penalty kill. I was being serious. So the next fight he got into, there were *no* theatrics, and right after that I put him on the penalty kill.

Another big difference in that second year in Norfolk was that I finally got a taste of the NHL. I saw Ryan VandenBussche and Aaron Downey playing at the top level the year before, and I'm thinking, *F—k, I've played against those guys. I can do that!*

To be completely honest, when Al MacAdam told me I didn't have to fight every night, I *heard* it, but I was still trying to establish myself in the AHL at that time. It was different back then. I had almost 360 penalty minutes that second year in St. John's. The NHL was different back then too, and I thought I could fight my way into the league. I wasn't quite at a place where I could take Al's advice and do something with it. It wasn't easy to balance that. By the time Yawns was telling me a similar message, I had established myself and was better able to hear it.

Norfolk and Virginia Beach was just a totally different environment than St. John's. It was laid-back! After practice we would go to a bar called Croc's, where there was a sleepy, surfer town vibe with live music. It was certainly not the type of atmosphere that I had experienced up North. Where St. John's offered Celtic music, beer, and cold weather, Norfolk was just a lot mellower.

There was a huge military presence too. We got to tour the ships and go on bases, but we didn't really hang out at the same bars as the military guys. Every once in a while we would connect. There was always such a mystique and aura around the Navy Seals and Navy pilots, but we didn't really interact with them as much as we might have liked.

The biggest Navy base in the world is in Norfolk, but those guys would have been stationed and living in a different area of Norfolk than us. Everyone I ever knew around Norfolk talked about a bar called Hot Tuna, where Erin and I went the night of our wedding. That was more the military bar, but we didn't usually hang around as much on that side of town.

My second year in Norfolk was Erin's first year as a hockey wife. It was all new for her, and there was a lot of learning to do. I think that's why I took up golf again. I couldn't very well tell Erin I was going to Croc's to spend six hours with the boys. But we also had a very close support system there with all the wives living so close together. Lasse Kukkonen and his wife came to live with us for a while at one point. When we would go on the road, Lasse's wife would be with Erin. They had greyhounds, and Erin *loves* dogs.

Erin certainly had a support system there in Norfolk, but it was a change in our relationship so there were obviously some bumps in the road figuring all of that out. I'm not saying it was hard; it was just an adjustment for us. She was used to living in Oshawa and working a couple of jobs; now she was living in Virginia Beach and *not* working. She had to make all new friends. I was also going from being the consummate team single guy and hanging out with anybody and everybody whenever they wanted to coming home to my girlfriend after practice. It was great and we loved it, but there were some adjustments for both of us.

That come-to-Jesus conversation with Erin, in which she told me to figure out if I wanted to commit to being a professional athlete or not, happened the summer before we started living together in Virginia Beach.

Before my first "date" with Erin, I had been in Toronto with my friends. I was at my buddy Hubie's place until six in the morning, drinking. After I had sobered up I jumped in the car and drove back to my hometown in Oshawa for my date with Erin. We were going to work out together. During that workout, I was reeking of whiskey before we went to have sushi for lunch. I ordered a roll and two Sapporos. It was my first weekend back home from Norfolk and there was a bit of the end-of-season "bender," I guess. But frankly, every weekend was kind of the same thing.

About a month later, Erin just said, "Alright, what are you doing here? If you're really serious about being a professional athlete, you can't live like this! You should have your fun, but you can't live like this." She told me I was just cancelling out all the hard work I was putting in every day. She told me I was the hardest-working guy she had ever seen, but it was all for naught. She told me I was just breaking even, and she was right.

If we hadn't had that conversation I doubt I would have two Stanley Cup rings right now. Part of it was the conversation, but part of it was my desire to impress her. I wanted to better myself to impress her. The conversation probably helped it sink in, and if that conversation had not taken place things probably would have worked out differently. If I hadn't done a 180, I wouldn't have gotten there.

Believe it or not, it was actually tough for me when I went from Norfolk to the NHL. When I was in Norfolk, I was up and down between leagues. My fourth year there I was actually up in the NHL for half the year, but I only played in 10 games with the Blackhawks.

I spent Christmas by myself in the hotel (and I would get to do *that* again later too). Christmas Day I just went to Dubliners, the bar across the street from the hotel. I sat there all by myself and drank about

15 Guinnesses, had a bite to eat, and went to bed. I think the bartender and I were the only two people in Chicago not celebrating Christmas.

The roster freeze happened on December 22 that year, and general manager Dale Tallon sent me down to the minors. That required me to go on waivers for more than 24 hours—it might have been 48 hours. He told me I was going to the minors, and I informed him I actually wasn't going down, because by the time I cleared waivers the roster freeze was going to be in effect. I told him he should have sent me down a day earlier.

I went out with Mark Bell and a few of my teammates and got fairly banged up. The next day was the team Christmas party, which I wasn't supposed to go to because I was being sent down. Assistant general manager Stan Bowman called me and jokingly said, "Thorty, I think you should work for me because you're better at my job than I am. You're right, we can't send you down. The Christmas party is at eleven o'clock—I'll see you there."

I showed up at the Christmas party and I saw Dale Tallon. I know Dale really well now, but at the time I didn't know him as well. He looked at me and said, "What the f—k are you doing here?" He was just busting my balls, but I thought he was serious and I got kind of hot. I was thinking, *I know you tried to send me down, but you don't have to rub salt in the wounds.*

After the Christmas party, I went to see Dale and Trent Yawney. I told them I hadn't seen my wife since October. It was my first year of marriage, and I don't think Dale even realized I *was* married. I asked if I could bring Erin in for the New Year's Eve party that was happening at our owner, Mr. Wirtz's, place. They said it would be no problem. They certainly couldn't see themselves doing anything before New Year's.

We had a game on December 30, I think against Columbus. Erin flew to Chicago from Toronto in the morning. I had a coffee with her and she went wandering around Chicago while I went to the pregame skate. I had lunch with her after practice then had my pregame nap. She went to the game, and after the game they sent me down. All I could think was, *Are you f—ing kidding me?!*

They told me Norfolk was playing in Wilkes-Barre, Pennsylvania, and that was where I was going. I said, "I'm not going to Wilkes-Barre. I'm going to Toronto with my family." They informed me I was under contract and had no choice but to report, so I asked if they could at least fly my wife back home. She flew back home on New Year's Eve day and I went down to Wilkes-Barre after seeing her for about an hour in the previous four months.

I met Norfolk in Wilkes-Barre, and the team hadn't even known I was coming. The trainers didn't even have my jersey with them. I certainly knew I didn't fly all that way, under those circumstances, to *not* play! The trainers went to a place like Michael's to buy stitching and lettering so they could make up a jersey for me. Mike Haviland was the coach, and he could see the look in my eyes. There was no way he was going to tell me I was sitting out.

I experienced a somewhat similar situation later when I was with the Anaheim Ducks. I was up with Anaheim and Erin was initially in Portland, Maine. Then she went back to Toronto when it seemed I might be up a while. They sent me down "on paper" a couple of times, but I was still with the team.

Sometime before Christmas, I went to Randy Carlyle and told him I wanted to fly my wife in for the holidays. He was honest with me, but it wasn't the answer I wanted to hear. He simply said he honestly didn't know what was going to happen with me. I might still be with Anaheim, but I might also be sent down.

It was shaping up to be another lonely Christmas, by myself, this time in Anaheim. Travis Moen and his wife, Amy, were nice enough to invite me over to their place for dinner. Travis and I were teammates and roommates in Norfolk, and this is the same Travis Moen who I would end up fighting a few years later when he was playing for the Montreal Canadiens.

I went to watch a movie that morning—I think it was *Borat*—then I went to Mo's for Christmas dinner. Around three o'clock I felt like I was intruding on their family Christmas, so I went back to the hotel. I bought a six pack of beer from the hotel lobby store and headed out to the hot tub. My plan was to have a soak, drink a few beers, grab something to eat, and go to bed. Another merry Christmas!

The Professional Bull Riders were competing for the week across the street at the Honda Center, and I ran into a PBR competitor. We struck up a conversation and spent a couple of hours in the hot tub. I asked him where he was from, and I'll never forget his answer. He was a true cowboy, and in his thick accent he said, "Well, my Mom had me in Oklahoma, but now I gets my mail sent to Denver." It was one of the most authentic things I've ever heard, and I've always remembered the line. I only wish I could remember the name of the cowboy who said it. I guess if I was going to spend Christmas by myself, at least I got something out of it.

I was thinking about the six-hour flight from Toronto to Anaheim, and I remembered what had happened to me and Erin in Chicago. I wasn't going to let it happen to her, or me, twice, so she didn't come for Christmas. I got to spend a second Christmas alone in a hotel room. Anaheim general manager Brian Burke came to see me after Christmas and just said, "The next time you want to bring your wife in for the holidays, come to me. Just speak to me. That's more important than the game sometimes." So I thought this was the time and asked if she could fly out for a week, and Brian let us do that.

Over the five years I was in Norfolk, I was up in Chicago for about 80 or 90 games, although I only played in 31. Brian Sutter was the Blackhawks' coach, and after the 2003–04 season he told me I was his fourth-line right wing. He said, "If I'm here, you're here." He told me to just make sure I got in shape and to be ready. Then the 2004–05 lockout happened. I didn't have a great year, and suddenly Sutter was out as coach and Trent Yawney was in.

I spent almost all of the 2005–06 season in Norfolk again. Chicago called me up for about 10 games. My contract was up and Anaheim offered me a chance to sign with them. After 15 games in Portland, Maine, I spent the rest of the season in the NHL, and played on a Stanley Cup championship team to boot. My minor league career was over. I never looked back.

TRENT YAWNEY
Head coach, Norfolk Admirals and Chicago Blackhawks

Bob Murray was a good friend of mine, and he was the vice president of hockey operations for the Anaheim Ducks. Bob had seen us play a number of times in Norfolk and when he and Brian Burke were putting that Cup-winning team together, they both liked tough, hard-nosed players. Bob took both Travis Moen and Thorty, who had played for me, and brought them to Anaheim.

CHAPTER 5

MICHEL, MONTREAL, AND ME

I'M NOT SURE I can even completely explain it, but I had the most torrid, heated rivalry there can be between a player and a coach with Michel Therrien. It all started in Granby, Quebec, in juniors. He was the head coach there. Peterborough played them in the Memorial Cup finals, and I didn't get a shift for the Petes the entire game. Therrien chirped me every stoppage.

I went to the Toronto Maple Leafs' training camp and we participated in an eight-game exhibition series against the Montreal Canadiens sponsored by Molson's that moved across Northern Ontario and Northern Quebec and into Newfoundland. Therrien by that time was the coach of the Fredericton Canadiens. Look, I was trying to make the team, so I was fighting a lot anyway, and every single game Therrien either had one or two tough guys in their system—or he was bringing guys up from a lower league—just to fight me.

Eight games straight, playing in small towns like Timmins, New Liskeard, Rouyn-Noranda, Grand Falls, Corner Brook—every single night I would get off the bus, walk into these tiny arenas, and fight two or three times. I think I ended up with 137 penalty minutes in like seven and a half games. It was unreal.

The final game of the series, I was coming up the ice on the power play, playing defense, and Therrien sent a guy off his bench who came on the ice without his gloves on. He came right at me, and I just snapped. We were trading punches, and I ripped his helmet off, shook him a little bit, and head-butted him. I skated off the ice and yelled to Therrien that he hadn't seen the last of me, and to just keep those guys coming.

I was playing for St. John's and we were about to be playing Fredericton something like 14 to 16 times a season, including exhibitions and playoffs. They had a bunch of tough guys, and I fought them all. Terry Ryan (who ended up being a teammate of mine), Sylvain Blouin, Dave "Moose" Morissette, Alain Nasreddine, Dion Darling, Brad Brown. I fought almost every game against Fredericton. You knew it was going to happen, and we had a tough team too, but it was like the Wild, Wild West back then.

I remember we were playing a regular season game—Fredericton against St. John's—but we were playing at the Bell Centre in Montreal. The Canadiens had just sent Moose Morissette down, and he was coming off a recent fight where he dropped Bob Probert. He had come from the IHL, and he was just demolishing guys. He had a brief stint with Montreal, and his first game down with Fredericton was going to be against us.

I knew it was going to be me against him that night, and I was a little more uncorked back then than I came to be, a little crazier. I was skating around during the morning skate, and the Fredericton coaches were up in the stands, watching us. I yelled up to Therrien, and he was just giving me that grin, so I screamed up to him, "You think you have someone for me? The first f—ing shift, just send him! Do you think I give a f—k?"

Sure enough, my first shift that night, Moose came out on the ice, and we squared off and I think we danced all the way down to the other end of the ice before we actually clinched. I used to throw lefts quite a bit back then, and then I would switch to the right. I knew Moose had a big right hand, and I just thought if I could beat him with lefty speed coming down the pipe, maybe I would catch him. I was wrong. Moose got the upper hand on me, for sure.

After we fought, we were sitting in the penalty box. Moose looked over at me and, "Thorty, what are you doing? Why lefts?" And I answered

I just thought I would try it. That's when he said, "You understand I'm a pretty tough guy, right? Try keeping your head up and spit with the rights when you're fighting a guy like me!" He was giving me some respectful advice. I was first or second in the league in fighting majors at the time, and I think in the back of his mind he had some respect for what I was doing.

He had just been sent down, and he was arguably one of the toughest guys in the AHL. I had certainly never seen him, and there was no HockeyFights.com back then so you could do a little pre-scouting. But I went at him head-on, and I think he respected that.

We ended up fighting again in St. John's maybe a month or two later. When we squared off, I was probably a little pissed about the first fight, and I couldn't allow him to have the upper hand. We had a pretty good fight, and I tagged him with a pretty good right. I basically did what he said and threw rights the entire time. I think I garnered his respect, and I think my teammates' too.

My first year I only fought 22 times, and 30 fights was not an uncommon number back in those days, especially for guys who were doing that for a living. I think maybe with that fight there was a turning point, and now I was *the* guy. I wasn't the supporting cast anymore behind guys like Clayton Norris and Greg "Bird Dog" Smyth. Now I was the guy who was going to be taking on the brunt of it. That kind of changed the outlook of my teammates.

Then we went into buildings, and I was going to be the guy. It didn't matter if it was Rocky Thompson or Dennis Bonvie or anyone from a list of dozens of names I could give you. Now it was up to me. It was also a pretty common theme that I was not going to be the bigger guy in most fights.

As I look back on it, maybe Michel Therrien was just joking around at the start, from that Granby-Peterborough Memorial Cup final when I didn't play. Now, I've never really been much of a fan of coaches who chirp, but he did, and I guess that was his prerogative. But I certainly wasn't going to just take it. And it grew and grew and grew from there.

In my second year with St. John's, we were playing Fredericton in the playoffs and we had a player named Mark Deyell who actually lost his eye. I'm not sure if it was true or not, but I heard a story that the players in Fredericton were told to not go visit Deyell in the hospital. It was playoff hockey, I guess, and whatever it takes to win. But I did not take kindly to that, and neither did a teammate of mine.

We were eating in a restaurant/bar the night before Game 5 in that series, and my teammate tried to fight Therrien in the bar. I had to grab Rollie Melanson, making sure no one else got involved. The next day the police showed up and people were questioned. The point is, the rivalry is truly *that* deep between us. At least for me.

It kept going. When I was in Norfolk, he was the coach in Wilkes-Barre, and again we played each other 14 times a year in the same division. They had Dennis Bonvie, Steve Parsons, Ryan VandenBussche, and David Koci, so what had happened between St. John's and Fredericton just continued between Norfolk and Wilkes-Barre.

TRENT YAWNEY
Head coach, Norfolk Admirals and Chicago Blackhawks

We played Wilkes-Barre 14 times one season, and they had a tough guy by the name of David Koci (6'6", 238 pounds). Michel Therrien was the coach and he would send Koci out just to fight with Thorty. Despite the size difference, Shawn was not going to back down from it, but he knew every time we played Wilkes-Barre he was going to have to fight Koci. I wanted Shawn to play, but Therrien wanted to eliminate Thorty as soon as possible. A lot of times it happened within the first minute of the game. Therrien sent Koci out there just for that specific reason.

So, of course, it just kept going into the NHL. I can't remember which team Therrien was coaching at the time, but he was smoking a cigarette in the coaches' room at TD Garden, and I got a couple of security guys to go tell him to put it out or they were gonna kick him out of the building. It continued when he was coaching in Pittsburgh and definitely when he was in Montreal.

And you wanna hear something funny? We finally talked about a year before this book came out. He was an assistant coach for the Philadelphia Flyers and I was in my current role with the Florida Panthers. I walked by him here in our building and he stopped me. He said, "You know what, Shawn? I respect you because you're just like me. I know we've had our differences, but I really, really respect you and respect what you've been able to do with the type of player you were."

I just told him I appreciated him saying that and we moved on. Now honestly, from those days back in the American League up until about a year ago I thought I would just f—ing punch him or choke him out if I ever saw him in the hallway. He didn't have a very long playing career and went right behind the bench, and maybe he had that same mindset, with his chirping, that made him more a part of the game. If I was behind a bench right now, I don't think I would say a word to a player, but everyone is different.

I never really played for a coach who chirped—a couple of assistant coaches, maybe, but they were fairly funny about it. Certainly not throwing daggers.

I grew up in Ontario, and Toronto and Montreal have almost as big an Original Six rivalry as Boston and Montreal. Montreal has a storied rivalry with both clubs, let's put it that way. If you grow up in Toronto, you don't grow up a Montreal Canadiens fan, so I never liked the Canadiens much anyway. Then I went to the Boston Bruins, with the rivalry between the Canadiens and the B's, and it felt like I was in St. John's playing against Fredericton again.

I don't necessarily remember my first Bruins game against the Canadiens, but I certainly remember that first playoff series. I remember Marc Savard being hurt by Steve Begin, and I remember the next year when I took care of that in Halifax in training camp. I also remember the Canadiens signing Georges Laraque, and Guy Carbonneau was coaching the team. They obviously remembered what had happened with Savvy and Steve Begin because Guy would have Big Georges out there.

I really respect Georges; he was a legitimate tough guy. I get anxious, but I'm not afraid of too many people. I had fought him four or five times before. I actually fought him when I was with Chicago and he was with Edmonton. He's a big and strong man, but I didn't approach him as being legendary status. You go toe-to-toe, and sometimes you get the better of him, and sometimes he gets the better of you. I mean no disrespect to Georges at all—in the context of people saying he was imposing, he was. But I can't be afraid of anyone and do what I did for a living. In my own head, I was the toughest guy to ever play the game.

I remember a media scrum after morning skate, and I said something along the lines of, "I could care less what *Guy* has to say," intentionally not pronouncing it "Gee." "We'll just figure it out tonight." So I knew it was coming.

The first shift, I went right after Georges. It was a fight. It was fine, but I wouldn't say anyone got an upper hand. He is bigger and stronger than me, and I would say he wrestled me a little better than I wrestled him. We each landed pretty much the same amount of shots, and then it was over. But the idea that a coach actually thought I would be intimidated by the idea of "wait until he gets here" is not the way my head operates. Especially when it's Montreal, and especially after already doing it for 14 years at that point.

There were certainly games when I would sit in my stall with the game notes, and think to myself, *I'm gonna have to go with this guy or that guy tonight.* I would certainly know who the tough guy was on their roster. I just never got too worked up about it. If I hadn't fought the guy before, that's when my nerves could get a bit jumpy. That's when I would want to get it out of the way, right away. If I had fought someone before, it didn't weigh on my mind too much.

Look, I'm human. There were definitely some nights when I might not have slept too well, thinking about it. There were some afternoon naps where I just lay there staring at the ceiling, waiting to get to the rink and get it over with. But by the time HockeyFights.com and sites like that started popping up, you definitely knew who everyone was and what they could bring. You knew who was coming, and you usually knew when it was coming. It was just part of the job.

I can honestly tell you there aren't too many tough guys I don't respect. I respect all of them. If you have to do that job for a living, you know better than anyone that it's just not easy.

I fought Eric Boulton something like 13 or 14 times, maybe more if you include a couple that we had in juniors. I respected everybody who has had to do that job. Whether we liked each other or not is probably a different story, but I respected everybody.

There were certainly some guys wearing a Canadiens uniform who I didn't like. I wasn't a fan of P.K. Subban, but that's fairly well known. I didn't know him off the ice; it was just the antics on the ice that always rubbed me the wrong way. He's a good player, but I always felt it was about the show more than anything with him. Hey, I was young, and I was all about the show at one point in my career too, so I try to see it from both sides. He used to drive me nuts, but I do love the work P.K. has done in the community.

There were a couple of others too, like Max Lapierre. There was a line brawl once, and one of the old-school refs, maybe Kerry Fraser or Paul Devorski, said to me, "Thorty, I can't let you do it." He knew I was just licking my chops. Then Max started chirping a little bit, and the ref said, "Max, one more word and I'm gonna *let* him do it!" The way he handled it was perfect. Max was like the dog who chirped, chirped,

chirped from the bottom of the stairs, then when you opened the door he ran back up.

Things can change, of course. Steve Begin became my linemate the year after we had a problem. He was a great guy! I had played a bunch against him in the minors. He was in St. John with the Calgary Flames organization and we had fought in the minors. I respected the way he played the game. I thought he just played a hard-nosed, tough game. He would never back down from anyone; he would fight outside of his weight class. He could skate, he was a great penalty killer, and he would block shots, so I really respected him. When he was on the Canadiens? Of course not! But he was a great teammate. I loved him.

Usually that first teammate meeting with a guy you've played against and fought against is pretty cordial. It's like, *Wow, I'm glad you're on my side now.* In Boston, we brought Brian McGrattan into camp, and I think I had fought him something like 10 or 12 times. We couldn't have had any more respect for each other.

I remember there was a lot of talk about how I wasn't big enough, and so they brought Brian in from Ottawa because Peter Chiarelli was looking for a bigger guy to do my job. He was being questioned about it by the media when he came to camp, and it was one of the most humbling things I've ever seen. I remember him saying, "Guys, my first year in the AHL Thorty kicked the s—t out of me! So let's stop talking about him not being a heavyweight!" I was established in Boston by that point, and he was there on a tryout trying to take my job, but he wasn't going to do it by chirping me in the media. Our last fight in the minors McGrattan cracked my orbital in a spirited tilt, so it definitely came around. That's the type of respect that most guys have for each other.

I've been hurt a few times in fights. Lee Cole hurt me in juniors, and I never got a chance to get back at him. That might be the only time I was really, really hurt in a fight. He was a little bit bigger than me, and he kept going after our star, Cameron Mann, so I went out to deal with it. We got the gloves off, and I don't remember much after that. He put my nose on the other side of my face, and I had to have surgery on it. That was also the only bad concussion I ever had in my career. I was out for a while after that. I'm not saying I never had any other concussions, but that was the worst. John Scott gave me a pretty good one, but I was running two days later. It just *looked* really bad.

John Scott was 6'8" and 270, pounds and he and Derek Boogaard were the only two guys I can remember being legitimately nervous about, because of their sheer size. I was fairly confident if I was fighting anyone 6'6" or below, because I have fairly long arms for my height and I could manage. But when you talk about 6'7" or 6'8", that's just a lot of height to give up.

We had a lockout that year and Buffalo signed John because of all the things that happened between our teams the year before. We had Milan Lucic running Ryan Miller and basically bullying the entire Buffalo organization, so they brought John in. But it was basically my job to fight the John Scotts of the world. I thought about that one for a long time. It ate at me.

After the lockout I knew we were playing the first week or two of the season. I called Tie Domi and asked for his advice. I wrestled with Zdeno Chara in the back of the locker room. The s—y part of having cameras everywhere is you can't practice for that stuff anymore without having to answer a million questions in the media about it. So I was grappling out back with Z and asking him what he doesn't like, what sort of advantage I could get with a guy that size.

Fighting was sort of an art form to me. By then, I had done it for long enough and I had enough training in it that it became a science. I had different ways of fighting different individuals and it was like martial arts. I always had a game plan, but I would adjust too if the game plan wasn't going the way I had hoped. I approached hockey fighting the same way people approach jujutsu. I always tried to be a step ahead, stay inside, know where the grips were, control the momentum, and control the weight.

So I wrestled with Z a little bit in the back room to figure out how I could get inside and how I could neutralize his height. Of course, it didn't work out the way I planned. I asked Claude Julien not to put me on the ice until John Scott was out there, hopefully at a stoppage. In my head, he was right-handed and threw very few lefts. He played right wing, so if I lined up on left wing, as soon as the gloves came off I could at least reach and grab for his right arm, because it would be right beside me. I thought I would just grab him with my left hand, then I would climb my way up to the top to his neck and at least control his right hand.

That was my game plan going in. Even if the game plan was executed, he still could have kicked my ass. Claude put me out there the third shift. The Sabres should not have been able to make the last change, but they did, and they put John Scott out on the ice. I was already lined up on right wing, so now his right arm was three feet away from me.

We got the gloves off. I missed my grab and I got caught without having his shoulder pad or his arm where I was looking to go, so I just tried to extend my arm. When he grabbed me, he missed his grab as well, and his fingers snuck through the ear loop on my helmet and twisted my helmet to the side. He was throwing punches, and I was surviving, but then he hit me behind my ear where my helmet would be. The helmet was twisted so he hit me twice in the soft spot behind the ear, and then he hit me on the way down.

I remember going to the penalty box, and I didn't have my feet underneath me, but I got there. I remember asking the penalty time keeper about five times how long until I was out. He just said, "You've got to get out of here." So he called the referee over, and they skated me to the runway behind the bench.

I went to the locker room, and I didn't feel *great* that night, but I actually thought I would feel a lot worse. I got home and went to bed. The next morning, Erin was supposed to fly back to Toronto to see her family, and I told her, "You know, I actually feel fine, so go on and see your family."

I didn't do much the first day—maybe binge-watched some stuff on Netflix. The next day was Saturday, and I actually felt *good*. I had brunch and then Danny Paille (who was also hurt at the time) and I went somewhere and watched the Bruins game in Toronto. I was actually back skating by Monday.

I called MMA star and UFC legend Kenny Florian, now retired, and I just told him, "Man, I got tagged pretty good behind the ear, but I feel okay." He made me feel a little better. He said, "Thorty, in MMA when we're kicking that's where we're trying to kick." He told me it causes more of an equilibrium problem than a concussion. I had such respect for Kenny, and this had happened to him a couple of times, so he really made me feel better about how things were going.

But the Lee Cole concussion was the worst. I was in the penalty box with a towel over my head, and I couldn't even look up. I was puking on the way home from the game. I didn't really know what a concussion was back then, but I took my time off after surgery and healed up. I think I was out something like four to six weeks, but a lot of that was waiting for my nose to heal. I had to wear a bubble for a while. I remember the doctor saying, "If you break this again, I'm not fixing it again." I just thought, *Well, this won't be the guy I go to next time, because it's probably going to get broken again.* I think it has been broken about another dozen times.

Fighting John Scott was something I wrestled with my entire career. We played them about a week later, and I just didn't think my head was ready. I think I was being cautious. I had the opportunity to go back at him a couple of other times, but by then I felt like I had proven myself enough in my career. I'm not afraid of anyone, and I'm not going to back down. If he had taken a run at any of my teammates, I would have 100 percent gotten my gloves off. And this is no disrespect to John Scott, but he was playing a minute-and-a-half a night and I was playing on what many people argued was one of the best fourth lines in hockey, playing eight to 12 minutes a night and contributing in many other ways. I didn't see the need to go sit in the box, and it might have been selfish of me to do it.

In my last season playing with the Florida Panthers, 2016–17, John had just been called up from St. John's in the AHL. He lined up beside me. Our coach, Gerard Gallant, told me he had talked to Michel Therrien and Therrien had told Gerard, "Look, we just called this guy up because he was an All-Star and he's retiring at the end of this year, so this is really a bit of a send-off." Gerard told me that I didn't have to do anything with him.

We were going to the playoffs, and he was getting ready to go away, and he asked me late in the game if I wanted to get the gloves off. I was just getting ready to congratulate him about the All-Star game and how happy I was that he got that recognition, but when he said that I just thought, *You know what, f—k you!* I told him he was an idiot and skated away.

I was truly happy for him with the All-Star thing. It might have started as a mockery, but the players who were there told me how happy they were that a guy who did what we did for a living was getting that recognition. It started with selecting one of the least skilled guys in the league and ended with Patrick Kane saying, "This guy protected me for years. I'm happy to be out here with him."

All the skilled guys in that game had a guy like John on their teams protecting them and allowing them to play the game the way they needed to. In that respect, I loved it. It didn't mean I wanted to get picked the next year, but I was happy for him. It allowed the skilled guys to say, "It's guys like this who let us do our jobs." There was a lot of noise about getting rid of that part of the game at the time, and the skilled guys stuck up for us.

Then you've got the whole thing about fighting with a shield or *against* a guy wearing a shield. I was certainly never trying to whack a guy in the shield with my bare hands. I was either trying to get the helmet off, or trying to hit him in the chin. I made a conscious effort to never hit a shield, but it happens.

We started off here talking about Michel Therrien, the Montreal Canadiens, and me, and then we dove down the rabbit hole to many other places. Kind of like my career. And next up for me was Boston.

CHAPTER 6

SHIPPING UP TO BOSTON

I SPENT A LOT OF TIME moving back and forth between the AHL and NHL. I started 2006 in the Anaheim Ducks' minor league system, but I was with the team for the rest of season, and that mattered most I won my first career Stanley Cup.

But right after the celebrations, I found myself on the market as a free agent.

Actually, Anaheim offered me a one-year deal, but my agent had a feeling I would have some other offers. Dale Tallon wanted to bring me back to Chicago. Chicago made an offer, for actually a little more money than the Boston Bruins, but for only a two-year deal. The San Jose Sharks said they were going to make an offer, but they were wrapping up Joe Thornton's and Patrick Marleau's extensions. They told me they were really interested but just needed a few days to take a look at everything. But that deal, if it happened, probably wasn't going to happen until July 2 or 3. I think there was one other team interested—maybe Buffalo—but the Bruins stepped up.

I told my agent, Anton Thun, to do whatever he could to get a three-year deal. I just wanted some security at that point in my life. Look, you're never really secure unless you have a no-move clause and millions in the bank, but three years was important to me. If I did my job, I was going to be there for three years anyway.

It was July 1 and I had already signed up for a charity fishing tournament about 40 minutes north of my hometown. I was the pseudo-celebrity in this fishing tournament. Hell, I don't even fish. I was just trying to do a friend of a friend a favor. We were out on the water and I didn't have any cell service.

Free agency opened up at noon and I was out on the water, and out of touch, until 2:00 or 3:00 PM. In that time, Cam Neely had called me and my agent was trying to get ahold of me. I got off the water and checked my messages, and my phone had been blowing up. I called my agent first, and he was kind of pissed at me. He said, "Alright, here are your options. Which way do you want to go, because I have to get back to these people ASAP!"

I was probably leaning toward Boston, but I asked him if he could get the money up a little bit. Chicago was offering more per year, so I wanted to see if Boston could match what Chicago had on the table. My agent was dealing with Peter Chiarelli, who was the general manager at the time.

Around 6:00 PM, we reached an agreement with Boston. I jumped in my Jeep and drove from Oshawa to Anton's office in Markham, Ontario. I signed the contract, drove back to my home, and we were celebrating by 8:00.

I had called Cam back after I spoke to my agent. I had never even met Cam and had never talked to him at that point. Obviously, I knew who he was, but I'm not sure I even knew what his role with the team was at the time. But I knew he was Cam Neely! I was a little nervous.

When we spoke on the phone he said to me, "I've seen a lot of players come through Boston, and I think I know this town really well. I've seen players like you come to this town, and I've seen this town appreciate players like you. Players who play like you are loved in Boston, and you should seriously consider that when you're thinking about where you want to play. Because it does matter!"

That may have been the understatement of my career. I didn't truly understand it until I got there, but I came to understand it as I started playing there.

Someone once told me the situation was similar to P.J. Stock's. I know Stocker and he was the same sort of player as me. I'm actually not sure if hockey fans in Boston would like it as much if some 6'8" guy was out there beating the hell out of people. I'm not gonna call players like me and P.J. underdogs, but we were a little smaller in stature and willing to go out there and battle bigger guys.

I'm a little bigger than Stocker, but neither of us are 6'6"—we were out there fighting the guys who are 6'6"! We wouldn't back down to anybody. It's in the nature of that town, it's in their DNA—they just don't f—ing back down to anyone. And they appreciate that in their players. They appreciate that we might not be the biggest, baddest men on the planet, but we're willing to take on the biggest, baddest men on the planet.

Take a guy like Terry O'Reilly. He would fight until he died, and I kind of know that feeling. You think of Stan Jonathan, who was certainly not a big man, but he played with a big heart.

I've always wondered what drives the city of Boston. Maybe it's the rivalry with the bigger cities, like New York, and the underdog mentality that builds. Maybe it's the individual towns and boroughs around the city of Boston, like Charlestown, Southie, Dorchester, and the way people were brought up. As long as you let them know that you're willing to get in there, they're always gonna appreciate you and let you know that.

Cam told me all about that, but I didn't appreciate what it all meant right away. I probably figured it out when I fought Riley Cote for the first time as a Bruin. A day or two after the game, I was at a Dropkick Murphy's concert and then the after party with Andrew Ference, and lead singer Ken Casey came up to me. Now, I knew who the Dropkicks were, and I was a really big fan, but Ken came up to me and said, "Holy f—k, kid, you're a f—ing animal! I f—ing love that!" When you have the founder of a band you're a fan of telling you you're a f—ing animal, that was great.

He was asking me for my phone number and telling me we had to hang out, and I suddenly thought, *Holy s—t! They really do appreciate this in this town!* Usually you get a simple, "Hey, good fight. Good job." But Ken Casey kind of embodies what a lot of Boston is really about. When someone like that, with that kind of passion, sings your accolades *to your face,* it makes you think, *Maybe I'm home.* We've become great friends and gone on golf trips together. I've been honored to help out with Ken's fundraising efforts on behalf of the Claddagh Fund.

Just walking around Charlestown, walking around Boston, you could feel it. When I would go into the Warren Tavern or the Ironsides—the places I used to hang out—there was a general appreciation for the job you were doing. The people are all blue-collar. It almost feels like they all grew up in Oshawa, right along with me. It felt like I was home.

MATT CHMURA
Vice president, Boston Bruins

We knew we had a problem and we needed to reconnect with the fan base in a lot of ways. We knew Shawn was the kind of guy who was going to give maximum effort, day in and day out. We also knew that that's what would connect with our fan base more than anything. That "tough, in-your-face, hard-to-play-against" brand of hockey was what our fans wanted. An honest effort. Then we did NESN commercials with guys like Shawn and Looch [Milan Lucic] showing that blue-collar, hardworking ethic, and we knew Bruins fans would relate to that. We didn't have results to sell to our fans at that point, but we knew what we had with guys like Shawn and Andrew Ference and Looch and others. We talked to Shawn about that, and he embraced that role. In fact, he embraced it so much that for a while he was the only guy living in Boston year-round. There was a mutual respect there—from Shawn to the fans and from the fans to Shawn.

When I signed in Boston, Erin and I sold our house in Oshawa. We had heard so much about the city and how great the people were. We knew we had to put up with the winters, but we decided to just embrace the culture of the city. Erin and I lived in Boston year-round, and we really got to know a lot of great people. It gave us a pretty good feel for the DNA of the city, and we learned that Cam's statement certainly was an understatement.

Then, of course, we had to figure out where to live. We looked at 33 houses in three days! Kevin Caulfield, our real estate agent, used to play hockey at Boston College and was a teammate of Jeff Farkas at BC. Jeff and I played together in the Maple Leafs organization. Let's just say Kevin was a very patient man. But he also knew he was getting a sale after three days of work. We looked all over. We looked in the South End, and we looked in the North End, but that was a little too expensive for us.

We liked the fact that Charlestown was in the city but had its own sense of community. We're from Oshawa, which has a population of 100,000 people but really acts like a small town. We loved the proximity to the Garden. I could jump on I-93 to get to the practice rink and could be there in 20–25 minutes. I didn't have to wait in the tunnel or carve through the city. I could walk to the Garden if I wanted to.

The biggest thing was location, but we found a place with quite a bit of square footage for downtown. It had a roof deck and had recently been remodeled. So we were sold. We loved the place then, and we still love the place today.

I'm not gonna lie to you; when I signed with Boston, I didn't know the first thing about the team. I didn't know one person on the team. I had played against Marc Savard in juniors, but it was probably one of the few teams I didn't know a single soul on. I hadn't even played against the Bruins with the Ducks the year before. I missed that trip with Anaheim because I was down in the minors. I truly didn't know one thing about the Bruins, and I didn't do any research on them either. This decision was based on the fact I had a chance to play in the NHL, I had a three-year deal, I had been told it was a city that would fit me very well, and that was it. Now, fortunately, I'd had the chance to win the Stanley Cup a few months earlier, so at 30 I wasn't chasing getting my name on the trophy. I was so lucky to already have that, so I wanted to find the best life fit. I was just happy to be there.

If the hockey wasn't what I hoped it would be, I just remembered that losing in the NHL is a lot better than winning *every* game in the AHL. That's all that mattered to me at that time.

I arrived in Boston with a little over a full season of NHL experience between all my teams combined. But I had always been a leader in the minor leagues. I was assistant captain in my second year in St. John's. I was one of the captains in Norfolk. I was the captain in Portland for the brief stint I was there before I got called up to Anaheim. I was told I was a captain in Norfolk because I was a great leader, and they wanted me to help with the younger prospects that Dale Tallon was bringing in.

In Anaheim, there were so many older guys with more experience and great leadership. I certainly wasn't a leader in that room. I was a follower because that was my role at that point.

I remember getting to Boston and kind of feeling my way through for the first few months. We had certain leadership groups with certain sub-captains...guys like Patrice Bergeron, Zdeno Chara, Marco Sturm, Glen Murray, P.J. Axelsson. I was in the Bergy group, and he wasn't doing a lot of the talking at that time. He was only 22 years old, and I remember him saying, "Thorty, you're the only guy in this group with a Stanley Cup. I need to hear more from you. You're the only one that's ever been there!"

I didn't want to come in a dressing room and try to take over, but that's when I decided, *Okay, I can do that.* I probably didn't really get into that role until about halfway through that first season. It certainly grew as I played there and became more of a fixture in the room. But after Bergy said that, I thought, *S—t! I've played 11 years pro now, and now I have a Stanley Cup. I don't have a ton of games in the NHL, but I have a lot of experiences that other people don't have.*

My first impression of Patrice was he's just a good guy. Then I learned about his work ethic; his talent level, which is through the roof; how quick he was; how he battled on pucks. My appreciation for him grew over the years because I learned what was in his DNA. When I first saw him at age 22, I could have just chalked it up to talent and trying to make a name for himself. Now I see a man who is thirtysomething years old, and he approaches every practice and every game the exact same way.

He hasn't aged. He's almost perfect in every way and with every single thing he does. It's how he approaches life in general, including the game. He may have been a 22-year-old kid at the time, but he had already played four years in the NHL. He played in the minors during the lockout year, so I got to see him, and I knew he was talented. He is the consummate professional.

PATRICE BERGERON
Bruins teammate

Shawn was a big part of our leadership core. It's something I mentioned to him a few times. I think at times he didn't completely understand how big of an impact he had on our team. People look up to him. His presence, his attention to detail, and his overwhelming desire to win were things younger players try to emulate. I told him, "People listen to you. They listen to your voice. Don't forget that people look up to you."

I used to joke that even though I was 31, Marco Sturm was a year younger than me, and Bergy was nine years younger than me, both of them were more mature than me. They knew more than I did, and I was older than both of them.

You look at that team my first year in Boston. You had guys like Jeremy Reich, Andrew Ference, Zdeno Chara, Milan Lucic—this team was tough! I remember my first meeting with Peter Chiarelli, and he told me he had asked Brian Burke about me. Burkie told Peter, "This guy is super tough, but don't rely on him to be the super heavyweight." Peter told Burkie, "Well, I don't need him to be. I have the biggest guy in the National Hockey League back on my blue line!" People forget that Z was the big monster back there. He is as tough as anyone who had ever played the game, but you forget because he's winning the Norris Trophy at the same time.

Looch was just a rookie that year, and don't forget about Mark Stuart; he was really tough too. Looch and Stewie used to come to my house after almost every game. My wife used to feed them, and I tried to take Looch under my wing his first few years. I tried to teach him when and when not to do it. He developed into a way better player than I ever dreamed of being. He didn't have to just do my role.

MILAN LUCIC
Bruins teammate

I'm not gonna lie—the first time I saw Shawn, it was kind of intimidating. He has just won the Stanley Cup with Anaheim, and he hadn't even shaved a lot of his playoff beard. He had the big beard going, and he's always been one of those guys in shape and jacked up, so I just thought, *Holy smokes! I better stay out of this guy's way!*

People don't remember, but we were linemates for about the first 40 or 50 games of my rookie year. Glen Metropolit played center for us, and he probably felt 10' tall and bulletproof playing in between us. I was a rookie and trying to make a name for myself, but Shawn had finally been able to sign a three-year, one-way contract, so he was trying to establish himself as an everyday player in the NHL. I think we kind of used each other to motivate each other.

We *did* have a really tough team my first year in Boston. And we made a conscious decision—Z, Looch, Andrew Ference, Shane Hnidy, and myself—that Boston appreciates a certain style of play. The city has an identity; it always has. We decided that the team should adopt that identity. We're not going to win every game, we're not the best team in the league, but we're gonna scrape and claw for every single point. When we're losing, we're gonna make the other teams f—ing miserable!

Just look at that first year. We had 12,000 people at the home opener. By the end of the year, we were selling out the building. We were in eighth place, but fans in Boston suddenly realized that the big, bad Bruins were back, and we started selling the place out. It wasn't because we were killing teams and blowing people out. We just adopted an identity that the city really appreciated. Then, of course, we got to play Montreal in the playoffs, and everyone in Boston knows what that means.

SHANE HNIDY
Bruins teammate

Shawn was part of that group trying desperately to change the Bruins' culture. You have to develop a core, but if you want to be a successful team it's about instilling habits. I remember that first year how f—ing hard we had to work, just to compete in a game. It was a grind. We weren't going to win games 6–5, we were going to have to win 2–1 or 3–2. And we needed everybody! Z was still learning at that point how to be a captain and how to be a leader. Bergeron was young and not really playing a lot yet. P.J. Axelsson was very influential on that team. The work habits got

81

developed that year, along with a sense of accountability, and those things stuck going forward. And we were tough! We stood up for each other. I know the game has changed, but Thorty and I just felt it was important to have each other's back, and stick up for one another. We weren't going to be pushed around—by anyone!

We *did* make a conscious decision that our identity was going to be the identity of the city. We were like a marketing tool, and none of us really knew the first thing about marketing. We didn't know a thing about our "brand;" we just kind of adopted it.

There were a couple of guys on that team who were kind of ending their Bruins runs when I was just beginning mine. P.J. Axelsson is *still* one of my best friends. I still talk to him and he's one of my favorite human beings. Glen Murray was also one of the best teammates ever. Muzz was a great leader, he had complete control of that room, and he had seen a lot. I relied on both of those guys a ton.

If we were on the road for dinner 10 times, I was probably with Axie eight of them. He was a tough Swedish SOB. He battled, he blocked shots, he fought for space, he was a great penalty killer. He was a skilled guy growing up, played on Olympic teams, but he adopted whatever role you needed him to. If you wanted him to play on the third line, he could. If you wanted him to play on the fourth line and help young guys out, he would do that. You could put him on the second line, or on the power play every now and again, and he could do that too. He was happy every day he showed up to work, no matter what role he was thrown into. I think that's something that guys really took to and learned from.

We went to New York one time, and Axie had the tightest white shirt and the tightest white pants, and red shoes. I said, "Axie, what the f—k are you wearing?" He just said, "It's f—ing New York, buddy! That's what you do!" I love that guy.

I had a lot of young roommates on the road those first few years. Travel isn't easy sometimes, with all the games, late nights, and time changes. I would ride them some times. They would tell me how tired they were and that I just didn't understand, and I would say, "No, I don't! I was working in a steel factory when I was your age! I wasn't making a million dollars a year, I was making twenty an hour, so I don't get it!" Working in a factory and 600 AHL games gave me a different appreciation than others maybe. I always tried to preach that and hold people accountable.

MATT CHMURA
Vice president, Boston Bruins

We were playing golf one day. It was me, Shawn, Michael Ryder, and Phil Kessel. It was a beautiful sunny day, and Phil was complaining about having to wear sunglasses. And Shawn was *all over him!* He was saying, "Yup, 75 degrees and sunny, and having to wear sunglasses! If you make $3 million dollars, it probably costs you $750,000 in taxes! What a terrible life!" And we were all laughing. He was coaching Phil in life, but I'm not sure if Phil understood that at the time.

I played against Marc Savard in juniors, but I really got to know him when I played with him in Boston—his vision and how he saw the game. He saw it three steps ahead of everyone else out there. He had incredible passing ability, but he also had a sneaky hard shot. He was a remarkable talent, for sure.

I only got to play 58 games that first year in Boston. I broke my foot fairly early in the season, and I was out six weeks. We were playing against Ottawa and Wade Redden did it. It was just a wrist shot and it hit me on top of my skate, and I didn't think anything of it. I just thought it was sore. I got it X-rayed in the machine they had in the back of the dressing room, and they found nothing. We flew to Buffalo and I skated on it the next day in the pregame skate. When I got off the ice, it was a whole other level of pain. When I got back to Boston, we got an MRI and found out it was fully displaced.

I remember telling trainer Don DelNegro that it could be broken, and he told me to get an X-ray. Then the X-ray came back negative, but after a couple of days I told Donnie that I just couldn't skate on it anymore. Hell, I couldn't even walk on it. Six weeks later, I'm back on my skates!

I had a short off-season because of winning the Stanley Cup with the Ducks, and I had put on 10 good pounds because I knew I was going to be relied on to fight some of the big boys. Anaheim had relied on George Parros for that. I was the second guy there, but in Boston I knew I was going to be the guy. I had put on some size, so I probably wasn't skating as well as I should have.

But after I broke my foot, strength coach John Whitesides got me in better shape than I was going into training camp. I felt better coming off a broken foot than I had going in. It doesn't make much sense, but I took six weeks off and felt better on the other side.

After the season ended, Erin and I spent our first off-season in Boston. That meant a lot of time at Fenway Park. In fact, at one point my wife and I had badges so we could buzz in and out of Fenway. I think they got sick of us asking for tickets! Sarah McKenna, Sam Kennedy, and Larry Lucchino were so amazing to us. Then I became friends with a few of the guys, so we were at Fenway a lot.

I even got to take batting practice twice at Fenway Park. I came to the conclusion that I'm not very good at baseball. But if you've got a chance to hit at Fenway, you've got to do it!

Erin and I developed an entirely new appreciation for Boston. We were still making lifelong friends. We loved it—we really did. There was a little bit of golfing for me. We were still trying to make our way around because when you play the season there, you're just really focused on where you have to be and what you have to do, mainly involving hockey. We would go back home for a little bit here and there, and check in on our families, but Boston was quickly becoming our home. We came to understand why people fall in love with living there.

LOUIE DeBRUSK
Admirals teammate; analyst, *Hockey Night in Canada*
Shawn was popular wherever he played, but he was meant to be a Bruin. He *was* a Bruin. Boston loves their tough, hard-nosed players and Shawn just fit that team and that town. I thought he would be perfect there, and that was even before he helped win a Cup. Then he became a Boston legend!

Thanks to my friend Sarah McKenna of the Red Sox I even got the opportunity to do "'Twas the Night Before Christmas" with the Boston Pops on opening night. Someone from the Sox had done this the year before, but for some reason no one was available. Sarah told the people at the Pops that the NHL was in a lockout, and while I would not normally be able to do it that time of year, I was available and could pull it off.

The last thing I would *ever* want to do is be up on a stage in front of that many people, narrating a story that I don't even know and keeping pace with an orchestra—the most famous orchestra in North America! But how many people get asked and how many people ever have that opportunity? So you do it. I was so nervous! While my parents had read the story to us when I was a kid, I didn't really know it all that well. So I downloaded a copy on my iPad, and for about two days I listened to it everywhere I went. If I was on my way to a skate, boxing, or anywhere else, there I was, practicing "'Twas the Night Before Christmas."

Well, wouldn't you know it, I completely screwed it up the day of inrehearsal! I'm sure the people at the Boston Pops were too nice to say it but were wondering if Sarah had steered them wrong. Thankfully, the performance went better, and I got through it pretty well. You can probably find it on YouTube. I made it. I didn't screw it up. Look, I wasn't that animated, but I was there and I got through it.

By the time we got into my second year in Boston in 2008–09, we had a number of young guys making their way onto the team, and I probably felt more comfortable with a leadership role. We were like one point out of the President's Cup and we ultimately lost to Carolina. Our record was 53–19–0–10. That's ridiculous! I mean, we should have won the Cup that year, but we still had some learning to do. It was a good group of guys, and I think I *did* feel like I was more a part of what was going on and of the leadership group.

We had a few new players on the team, as you do every year. I remember the first day of camp we had fitness testing in the morning, then we had a full team meeting out at the Marriott in Wakefield later in the day. Cam was scheduled to talk to the team at 2:00 PM, followed by Peter Chiarelli. Michael Ryder walked in at like 2:15. And Cam said something like, "Rydes, a little late, huh?" Michael just said, "Yeah, I got lost." And Cam looked at him, and he had a Starbucks cup with like 18 f—ing letters on the side of it, and Cam said, "But you had time to get a coffee, huh?" He had obviously sat at Starbucks for 20 minutes waiting for his latte to be made, so he was late for the first meeting of the year. That was actually a common theme for him. I love that guy, but he wasn't on time very often.

It was also my first opportunity to get to know Mark Recchi, who was 40 years old when he arrived. It was amazing. What an amazing guy. After he was traded to Boston he came into the locker room, and just the week before I was on the ice in warm-ups in Tampa chirping him about his hair. I was telling him he should just shave it and get it over with. He came into the room the next week and he said, "Thorty, my daughters actually love my hair! I know I should shave it, but it's not my call!" All I could do was apologize to him.

He came in and actually taught us what it was going to take to get there. The way he approached the game, he was like Bergy. Every single day he showed up and was the hardest-working guy at practice. It wasn't like he felt he had to be, it was just the way he was wired. He just didn't know any other way, and that's why he became so great. He was a superstar for a lot of years and didn't rely on being a superstar to carry him or us.

I remember him saying to me one night, over a couple of beers, "Damn, I'm 40 years old, Thorty! I used to be able to put the team on my back, and just go, but I can't anymore. I need other guys, and I'll tell you right now, I'm going to teach them how to put the team on *their* backs!" He just gets it. He's a winner and he's a f—ing leader.

I didn't know how many years I was going to get to play with him, but he just kept coming back, and we were *so* happy to have him. He taught us so much about leadership. I think he even taught Z about leadership, to be honest. He taught him how to loosen up a little bit and understand that everyone has their ways. I sure learned a lot from him.

He was as patient as could be with the younger guys, and he would really try to teach them, but then he would also hold them accountable when they needed to be. He had such a good emotional IQ and really used it to his advantage when approaching the dressing room and the game.

Rex has certain attributes, as we all do. I think all of the Bruins leaders had their own strengths and weaknesses. I hold people accountable a lot more. I was a lot more vocal than others. I think Rex was kind of between me and Bergy. Look, I worked my ass off, but I'll admit I gave up on pucks at practice from time to time. Those two never gave up on a puck—ever!

Rex spoke up whenever he felt he needed to speak up, and probably more often than Bergy. I haven't played with Bergy for six years, so he may be completely different now than he was then. He also didn't need to talk, because we had a lot of guys who did. Bergy led more by example and spoke when he had to.

PATRICE BERGERON
Bruins teammate

I always thought Shawn had much more hockey talent than he was ever given credit for. He could actually play defense for us if we needed him to. He understood the game and was very intelligent. When we needed energy, he sensed that and found a way to provide it. That didn't always mean dropping the gloves; sometimes it meant going for a big hit or providing an important shift. He could always read the bench, he could read the time and place and exactly what was needed. In the dressing room it was the same thing. He held guys accountable.

Rex had the experience; he had the Cups. He had the amazing IQ and he had the work ethic. He also had the patience, so there wasn't anything I ever felt he was lacking in the leadership department.

But you might be surprised that Rex isn't the guy who just captures the room the minute he walks through the door. He's such a personable person; he's the guy who will go out and have a beer with you. He doesn't walk in and *demand* a presence. But he's the guy everyone wants to go to war for...and with.

My second year with the team I finished second in penalty minutes to Milan Lucic. I think the last game he took another two or something. But honestly, I never cared about leading the team in penalty minutes, nor did Looch. I did it when I had to. It was quite the opposite actually. I never took that many minors for two reasons—I never wanted to put my team down for two minutes, and I wasn't sure if I would ever get another shift if I took a minor!

MILAN LUCIC
Bruins teammate

Think about it—Shawn Thornton, with his Irish roots, and playing the way he played—was perfectly made for playing in Boston. I still have that poster that they made up of me and him that just said BRUISE BROTHERS. I've moved a couple of times in the last couple of years, but that poster always goes with me. It's somewhere safe. I just couldn't be happier that I had someone like him by my side, and I couldn't be happier for him and the success he's had. He was always about culture and putting the team first. Shawn had no issues about calling you out. It wouldn't have mattered if you were Z or Rexie or Bergy, or a guy that just got called up from the American Hockey League. If you weren't putting the team first, Shawn had no problem coming up to you and putting you in your place.

When you only get 12 to 14 shifts a game, you don't want to miss one because you're sitting in the box serving a minor. For some of the guys playing on the first, second, or third lines, they can take an aggressive penalty because they never have to worry about being benched for it. But if I take a minor I might not get back out there. I'm pretty sure that on every team I was ever on, I led the team in major penalties, but not necessarily in overall penalty minutes. Look, if you get in 36 fights there's a pretty good chance you're going to lead the team in PIMs!

We had laid the groundwork. We were ready for what was next, and the best was yet to come.

CHAPTER 7

THE PITTSBURGH PENGUINS AND ME

EVERYONE ALREADY KNOWS THAT if you play for the Boston Bruins, your big rivalry is with the Montreal Canadiens. It seems kind of natural that any emotional issues you'd have would be with the Canadiens, and I certainly had those too. But for whatever reason, it seems like a couple of the biggest stories of my career involved the Pittsburgh Penguins. It's even hard for me to explain, but it's true.

The first was one of the most famous confrontations between the Bruins and the Penguins, and it probably led to the end of the career of one of the most talented guys I've ever played with, Marc Savard. I opened with all the details of this whole story to start this book.

The second had to do with the only suspension of my career, and maybe the most emotional I've ever been about something that happened in the game. I've always said it's the thing I'll take to my f—ing grave.

We were playing the Penguins on December 7, 2013. Brooks Orpik laid a pretty tough hit on Loui Eriksson. Whether it was questionable or not was up for debate, but it really didn't matter to me. One of my teammates was on the ice, and Brooks was challenged, first by myself and I think by Dougie Hamilton too. Brooks wouldn't answer the bell with either of us. Now, it ended up that Loui was out for the next six weeks with a concussion, but we didn't know that at the time of course.

I had known Brooksie for a long time, and we were actually friends. We skated together in the off-season and we rode the train down to NHL lockout meetings together—as I said, I've known him for a long time.

So the hit happened, and he didn't respond immediately. A couple of shifts later, I get on the ice, we're playing, and the whistle blows, and I turn around and see Brad Marchand laying on the ice, hurt. Now, I have a job to do, and two of my teammates have been hurt in the last six to eight minutes, and *it has* to be addressed. It's my job.

I look up the ice. One, Brooksie is the biggest guy on the ice, and two, he had already hurt a teammate, so I grabbed him.

My side of the story—and I know people will say I'm biased—but I'm gonna tell you what I believe, wholeheartedly, in my head. I grabbed Brooksie from behind, and I won't even say I threw him to the ice, because in the moment and when I watched the video, I made sure his head didn't hit the ice. I held him up a little bit. In my mind, I was going to rough him up a little with my glove for a few seconds and I thought I was going to get a two-minute minor, maybe four. I purposely kept my glove on. Then it's addressed—I punched a buddy of mine in the head and kept my gloves on. I'll go the penalty box for four minutes and then probably have to fight their tough guy later in the game. It's addressed, it's over. But it didn't turn out that way.

Brooksie didn't get up. I still can't figure out for the life of me how he was that seriously hurt. I've boxed half my life, and I know to a fairly accurate degree how heavy my hands are when I'm hitting somebody, and when I'm trying to hurt them. That wasn't the case with Brooksie. I feel like if my hands were that heavy I would have won every frigging fight I was ever in.

BROOKS ORPIK
Pittsburgh Penguins

My recollection of the incident probably had to do more with after the play. I was watching video of my hit against Loui Eriksson. People in Pittsburgh probably though the hit was okay, and people in Boston definitely thought it was a bad hit.

On the play that got Shawn suspended, I honestly think it was just a case of bad luck for both of us the way I fell. When you play the way we both did, there are always plays you would like do-overs on, but you don't get the chance at that. I know people think I'm crazy for saying this, but I don't think there was any intent on his part. It was totally emotion-driven and heat-of-the-moment type of stuff. Only Shawn can say what his intention was, and everyone else tries to guess or speculate, but I know what kind of player Shawn was.

I probably held bad feelings toward Shawn while I was dealing with the issues from the play. But I also think I moved on quicker than other people around me did. I'm not one to hold grudges, and there were plenty of plays during my career that I would like to take back if I could. That's just part of hockey. You can learn from certain plays, but you don't get to take them back. Guys who are more physical and guys who hit more have more of a chance for things to go wrong. I probably held a grudge initially, but it didn't last long for me.

The concussion wasn't actually that bad. I didn't have a super hard time with that, and it only affected me for a couple of weeks. But the neck issue I had a hard time with for a longer period of time. Optically, this issue probably looked worse than other things I had to deal with, but I've had other issues that affected me even more.

Brooks rolled, and he didn't get up, and that's my responsibility. It's my fault. I hadn't watched the video until my second disciplinary hearing, when I had to go through it almost frame by frame. The optics were just terrible. He was on the ice for a long time and got carried off. And to be honest, Brooksie and I have never been quite the same. We skated together again the following summer, and I actually went up to him and tried to hug him while I was naked to try and break the ice, but I'm not sure if that worked. He's a good guy, and I swear there was never malicious intent on my part.

I've done this thing a hundred times in my career. I've played on the line, but I had never, in my opinion, gone over the line. And it's not an easy line to ride when you're in my position. But it was never my intention to hurt that guy—at all.

BROOKS ORPIK
Pittsburgh Penguins

My experience with Shawn was that he was a very honest player. He played a hard game, but he played an honest game. When you play defense, you often have your back to the forward who is coming in on the forecheck. Shawn would always say my name. He would say, "Orrs, I'm coming! I'm coming!" You knew he was going to finish his check, but he almost gave me a chance to prepare myself and brace myself for what was coming.

I had to have a hearing with the NHL, and I was sitting across from some familiar faces. I was pleading my case to Patrick Burke, Brian Leetch, and Brendan Shanahan, who I had played against.

I feel like the first hearing was fairly contentious, and I never felt like my side was being heard. Look, I get that there are other factors; there was a lot going on in the atmosphere of hockey with lawsuits and things like that, where the game was going and the perception of my role within the game. But in the end, I got hammered. I was absolutely shocked that I got a 15-game suspension for a first-time offense.

I talked about it with Gary Bettman numerous times, and he said he appreciated how professional I was, under the circumstances. But I was surprised I got that many games, and that's why I appealed it.

And I've got to give the commissioner credit—he was nothing but unbelievably professional, upfront, and honest with me through the whole process. He called me, originally, to let me know what the suspension was. I was pretty pissed off that it got leaked to TSN's Darren Dreger, who ran with it without even giving me a phone call, like a decent human being should.

I remember I was boxing at LA Fitness with my buddy Tommy McInerney, and there was no real cell service in there. When I walked out, I can't even tell you how many messages I had. My phone just blew up after the Dreger report. So I called Peter Chiarelli, and I said, "Is this true?" He said he was still trying to find out and hadn't heard anything either. He called me back a few minutes later and said it was all true—I had been suspended for 15 games.

I went home, walked into the house, and I think Erin could read the look on my face. She asked what had happened, and I told her I was suspended for 15 games, and that I couldn't talk right then. I went upstairs to our bedroom, and I just broke down for about an hour. It probably took me another half hour to compose myself. I reached out to my agent and told him how pissed off I was to learn I had been suspended for 15 games on Twitter.

So I went through the appeal, and I can't stress again how professional Gary Bettman was.

Every year, we took a large group of sick kids to the movies over Christmas. We were at the movies and I went outside to grab a coffee and Gary called me to say, "Look, Shawn, before you hear it from anyone else again, like last time, I just want you to hear it from me that we are keeping your suspension at 15 games. You are more than welcome to appeal it, again, to a third-party arbitrator, and we understand if you want to. But I just wanted to call you myself."

Look, he's the commissioner and he doesn't have to make that call personally, especially during the holidays. He has people who can make that call, but it meant a lot to me that he did.

We get through the Christmas break, and at that point I had been out for almost four weeks. We were getting ready to go on the West Coast swing. I had to talk with Chiarelli, and I had to talk with Claude Julien. They were both very supportive and told me that if I wanted to appeal it again, then they thought I should.

But I just made the decision that four weeks had been long enough. If I went on this 12- or 14-day road trip, then I would be eligible to play on the last game of the trip. I just wanted to get ready to play, and the next hearing probably would have been during that road trip. I would have had to fly from the West Coast back to New York, then back. And I figured that to save a few thousand dollars, if I got a couple of games knocked off, then the juice just wasn't worth the squeeze at that point. I felt like it was making a point just to make a point. So I took my punishment and just moved on, and got myself ready for when I could get back in the lineup.

But that being said, I was *not* aware at that point that my pension was going to be affected. Those 15 games, when I turn 62 and a half years old, mean I lose almost a quarter of that season's pension. It wasn't just a few grand. This will affect me for as long as me and Erin live out the pension. I wish I had all of that information back then when I was making my decision. That would have probably changed things. I might have done the same thing, but I wish I had all the information at the time.

I had never had a hearing—hell, I don't think I had even ever had a game misconduct—so I went into this process a little bit blind. My agent tried to help me; he had a couple of players who had been through it. But the Players Association is in a tough spot because it is supposed to be supporting *both* players—my side and Brooks' side. Look, the PA was there and was somewhat sympathetic, but there's a bit of a conflict when it's you against another player.

I think I was prepared. I was nervous, but I went in and pleaded my case. I've heard some things from behind the scenes, about who was on my side and who wasn't, but I think I should keep those things to myself.

At the end of the day, I f—d up. It wasn't intentional, and I didn't mean it, but I f—d up. I paid the price, and I moved on.

I remember getting ready to come back; the practices were just brutal. The first four or five days, Don Sweeney skated with me. I remember showing up at our practice arena in Wilmington. It was just freezing, and there were barely any lights on. And if you know Sweens, you know he might be the best-conditioned athlete in the whole organization. I skated with him for three or four days, and it was the hardest I had ever skated in my entire career. I was thinking, *This is the assistant GM! My contract is in his hands!* You can't say "uncle," right?

I also remember coming home and saying to Erin, "I don't know how much longer I can do this. He's going to break me!" I was in pretty good shape, and I like to think I'm mentally tougher than a lot of people, but I was afraid Don Sweeney was going to break me. Sweens is the man! He does Ironman and Super Ironman triathlons. And he was doing most of these drills with me. He didn't do all of them, but he did most of them. And he always looked like he could go for another two hours. Jesus!

When the suspension finally came down, Donnie called me and said, "Look, Thorty, why don't you take a day, and then we'll get started." When I said thanks, I'll just take a day, it was really because I wasn't sure I could last another day on the ice with Sweens busting my ass on the ice again. So I took the day.

CHAPTER 8

THE COLLAPSE

(Ed. note: The Boston Bruins had a 3-0 lead over the Philadelphia Flyers in the Stanley Cup playoffs in 2010 and had a 3–0 lead in Game 7 of that series before falling 4–3 and being eliminated. What follows is Shawn's recollection of that playoff series—herein known as The Collapse.)

I THINK YOU CAN CHALK that series up to a few things. Losing David Krejci was huge, obviously. I'm not going to say he was underrated, but maybe a little bit. I think he was leading the league in playoff scoring at the time he got hurt, and he was obviously a *huge* piece of the puzzle for us.

But you get to Game 7, and you're up 3–0. I do think we had some people who became—*complacent* might not be the right word, but who perhaps took a 3–0 lead for granted. Look, you tip your cap to Philly. The Flyers did *not* pack it in. They kept fighting, and they were not discouraged by being down 3–0.

Part of the issue we faced was the situation with Marc Savard. It's always hard to place yourself back in that situation, because you are *so* focused on the here and now. I was trying so hard to be ready myself to play every game that I probably was guilty of not thinking too much of where Savvy was. We were all there to support him, obviously, but you're also focused on, *What the f—k am I going to do to help this team win?* But if he said he's good to go, then *let's go!*

I recently went back and looked at that playoff year, and if you gave me six guesses I probably still wouldn't have guessed who our leading scorer was that playoff year. And six is probably the magic number, because our No. 6, Dennis Wideman, led the team in playoff scoring that year. Of course, Krech was leading when he got hurt, but Wides actually led our team in playoff scoring that year. I might have guessed Nathan Horton or Rex or maybe Bergy, but I would *not* have guessed Wides!

But after that loss we went into the longest off-season ever. I love Boston, but I couldn't stop and get a coffee without hearing about it. I guess that's a blessing and a curse at the same time. The Bruins have great, passionate, and very knowledgeable fans. I think we were pretty approachable as professional athletes, but I don't think there was *one* day in the off-season where I didn't hear about it.

But I also truly believe that 2011 doesn't happen without 2010. I think that crushing defeat gave us the knowledge of how urgent *every* minute of a playoff game is. It fueled us for the next season, and fueled us for the off-season as well. We went into that off-season f—ing pissed, and we took that attitude into the next season too. I think we did a lot of things in the 2010–11 season the *right* way, and I think it absolutely helped with the success we had thereafter.

I also think the 2010–11 season was the real beginning of the Merlot Line. If you remember, at the start of the year it was me, Brad Marchand, and Gregory Campbell. We probably played together for the first 15 games or so. Daniel Paille was on the third line. But Marchy was playing unreal, and he got bumped up, so Claude put me, Soupy, and Danny together. I think Jordan Caron was kind of in and out of the lineup, so he had some time with that fourth line too, but it was the three of us for the majority of the season.

We knew each other's tendencies and we played so much together in practice and games that we really didn't even need to speak. It was a unique situation. Claude rewarded us with ice time, and I think it was the first time we played nine or 10 minutes a night on average. Some nights we were playing 13 or 14 minutes. There were nights when other lines weren't going, for whatever reason, and Claude rewarded us with extra ice time, and it helped us. Hell, I think it helped everyone on the team. The teams that win are the teams that have depth, and we proved that we gave the team depth that year.

We ended up being pretty popular among the fans. If the Bruins had won the Cup against the St. Louis Blues in 2018–19, maybe that fourth line would have toppled us as far as popularity is concerned. But we had the advantage of good marketing too.

We ended up calling the line the Merlot Line after a Super Bowl party that year. The NESN show *Behind the B* happened to catch the footage of Geoff Ward saying, "You guys are going tonight! We can't hang with a line like the Merlot Line after a party!"

We had a tagline, we had an identity, we ended up winning. We had guys fans found very relatable. Daniel Paille might still be one of the nicest human beings I've ever met, and he started to live in Boston year-round too. He'll sit down and talk for four hours with a complete stranger! Soupy played on a broken leg, and I fought for a living and had already established a brand there. It ended up being a quiet, perfect storm that we were all lucky to be a part of.

CHAPTER 9

2010–11 SEASON

WHEN I FIRST SIGNED WITH THE BRUINS, my very first exhibition game at training camp that year was in St. John's, Newfoundland, where I had spent a lot of very good time in the minor leagues. I mean, I'm not even sure how you make something like that up. One of my first road games with the Bruins was the home opener for the Anaheim Ducks, the banner-raising for the Stanley Cup championship team that I played on. Now, I'm pretty sure the NHL didn't do that to accommodate *me*, but it sure worked out pretty great. I was out there watching the banner that I helped win going up.

Fast-forward to the 2010–11 season. I found out during the summer that the Bruins were going to open the exhibition season in the country where my mom was born, so we were going to Ireland! We opened up in Belfast, where I had never been, and my mom had never been back since she emigrated to Canada when she was a kid.

So, of course, I offered to fly her over to Ireland to be there with us. She stayed with family, and I originally had her booked to be over there for four days, but she ended up staying for a week and a half! I think she got there and decided she might not want to come back.

It was so much fun for both of us. I got to catch up with, and actually meet, so many members of my family. My second uncle picked us up at the hotel and took us on our own personal family tour. We went to a pub in the outer ring of the city and saw so much. If I remember correctly, I ended up needing 42 tickets for our game in Belfast, most of them for my mom's immediate family. Many of them had visited in Canada over the years, like at Christmas or summer breaks. We got to see how they all lived on a daily basis, and it was such a great experience. I loved every second of it.

As you can imagine, there weren't too many descendants of Belfast playing over there, so they used my connection a little bit to help promote the game. Scott Waugh, one of our trainers, was out at a pub and someone came up to him and asked, "Do you know Shawn?" When he acknowledged that he worked for the team, he was asked, "Oh, did you know his family is from here?" I tried to fly under the radar, like I usually do, but I remember there were newspapers there when we got off the plane, taking pictures and stuff.

Owen Nolan was the first player who was actually born in Belfast to play in the NHL, and he was obviously a more high-profile player than me. I won't say he had a better career, because I *did* have a couple of Cups in there. But other than Owen I guess I was the next closest connection to Belfast, so playing over there was just great.

If I remember correctly, I think it was also the first game ever for the original Merlot Line. It was me, Greg Campbell, and Marchy, and we each had a couple of points in the game. There were a couple of guys I had played against in the minors on the other side, and I remember the building being packed. I loved it all!

It was clear right from the start that Brad Marchand could play at a high level. We had brought Soupy in from Florida, and he had played regularly on the third line there, so we knew he could play too. You maybe had an idea there was something cooking with the fourth line, but we still had a couple of exhibition games to go, and the start of the regular season, so there were still a lot of unknowns. We didn't even know if the lines would stick together that early in the preseason.

We left Belfast and moved on to Prague, and that gave guys like David Krejci and Zdeno Chara the chance to play in front of their friends and family. Plus, Andrew Ference had played in Prague in the previous lockout, not too far in the past, so he was also very familiar with Czech culture. Tuukka Rask had been there a bunch, and I had even been to Prague when I was around 17 years old with my Oshawa Midget team.

The team bonding that took place during that European trip was worth more than you could ever put a value on. It was priceless. You go on the road for nine days to start the season, in foreign countries. The time zones are all off, but you're all together, and you learn to get on the same page very quickly. There were zero distractions, so it was just all of us getting to know each other.

There is a limit to how much you can do when you're abroad like that and playing as a professional athlete, so you end up going to eat and drink at the same places, you're staying in the same hotel, you end up walking around the city and taking tours together. It was a great experience. I've told people this a million times, but I don't know if we win the Cup that year without that trip.

A lot of it is the intangibles that go on in a hockey dressing room—the camaraderie, the sense of family—because the guys are always together. Hockey players are inherently humble, so getting everyone together really works. I certainly don't mean that families are a distraction, but when you travel, you literally have nothing else to focus on except being a team.

There is always a huge team group text, and everyone makes plans together. We had a team dinner in Belfast, and a couple of us went down this little alley to a tiny pub with live music. After the game, I had my family there and got together with them for a while, but then I met up with some of the guys and had a few drinks together.

We had another team dinner in Prague. I can't remember who set it up, but the entire team was there, and we had a couple of drinks together after dinner. Those are things you just wouldn't get if you had training camp at home for the last week of the preseason. Guys, as they should, go back home and have dinner with their families at the end of the day, but we were forced to be together because of the circumstances, and I thought it was amazing for our club.

For a lot of NHL players, training camp and preseason suck. It's funny how things changed over the years. When I started, I was used to five-, six-, or seven-week training camps back in the day and many of the guys had to stay in hotels. My first year in Boston, Erin didn't come to training camp, because I didn't even know if she was allowed to. We were getting our house set up, and packing up our place back in Canada, but she wasn't there for really any of it.

But there were advantages too. Because I wasn't worried about being home at six o'clock for dinner with my wife every night, I went out to dinner with a new teammate every night or had them over to dinner at my house. I remember one time, I didn't even have all my furniture yet, but Mark Stuart, Jeremy Reich, and Nate Thompson all ended up just staying there until they could find places to live. I woke up one morning, and they were all sleeping on couches and in sleeping bags and on mattresses on the floor.

When you're a newcomer on a team, and it's your first training camp, those things are just invaluable. By my second year, Erin figured out that she was allowed to be there during training camp, so she didn't go back to Canada. But training camps used to be about just that—learning about each other and getting to know each other.

When I started in Toronto, the Leafs used to take training camp to neutral sites, places like Barrie, London, or Kitchener, for at least five to seven days, just so the team could get to know one another and focus on getting ready for the start of the season.

We came off our European trip knowing we were a pretty good team. The season before we had almost won the President's Trophy for best record in the regular season, and we had made a couple of adjustments in the off-season.

It probably took until the game against the Dallas Stars on February 3 before we proved to everyone what we felt in that dressing room. You've heard that old adage, "Don't poke the bear." We actually meant it. We felt we could play any type of game we wanted to. If you wanted to run and gun, we were fine with that. We could score off the rush. If you want to grind, we can grind. If you want to hit, we can hit. If you want to fight, f—k, good luck!

There is a whole chapter in this book called An Identity Is Born where I talk about that Dallas game in depth. But the important thing was we needed to send a message to the rest of the NHL that the Boston Bruins were for real, and we wanted everyone to know it. It wasn't just the three fights in the first minute of the game; it was the fact that Looch scored right after the fights, then we added another goal right after that. We were sending a message. Hell, I even put one past Stars goalie Kari Lehtonen before the game was done!

So we knew we were good, but for me, it wasn't until the moves we made at the trade deadline that I was convinced we were maybe good enough to win it all.

When Peter Chiarelli brought in Rich Peverley, Chris Kelly, and Tomas Kaberle, my perception just changed. We were on the Western trip, in Vancouver for five or six days, when he made those moves. All three guys joined us on the road, and sort of like the preseason trip I was talking about, we were all together and away from our families. We had the rookie dinner in Vancouver, and these guys got to see right away that we were a very tight team. Most of us had been around each other for three years at that point. But they came in and we got to know them and they got to know us. It was just hotels, practices, games, and where does everyone want to eat. That was it, and it was perfect for team bonding.

All three of those guys just fit in seamlessly. They embodied exactly what it meant to be a Bruin. They reflected the character that the team already had. All three were extremely unselfish and disciplined, with a team-first attitude. All had great careers, but they had such an impact on our team finishing up the regular season and into the playoffs.

We were in the middle of a winning streak, and they helped push it to seven straight wins. That was when I started thinking, *We're really f—ing good!* Tomas Kaberle was one of the top two defensemen in Toronto for the previous several seasons, and he was like our sixth defenseman in Boston, and on the second-unit power play. Now that is depth!

It falls on everyone in the room to make sure the new guys feel like they're part of the group. Usually there will be two or three guys on a team who would have played with one of the new faces. For instance, we brought Shane "Sheriff" Hnidy in at about the same time. He had played with us about a year and a half before that but had shoulder surgery and couldn't sign anywhere. Peter brought Shane in because of his leadership abilities, and he was just instrumental behind the scenes. Sheriff had played with both Kells and Pevs in Ottawa and Atlanta, so when he told the guys in the dressing room, "Fellas, both these guys are *our* kind of guys," it just broke the ice right away.

Other guys knew them from other teams too, so you felt like you knew who they were before they even got there. That Boston dressing room just welcomed new players with open arms, maybe as much as any team I've ever been on, and they became part of the family immediately. Hey, it's not easy to walk into a new room. I've been there and it's tough; it can be intimidating.

It always starts with the leadership, and everyone leads in different ways. I'm always full-go. I was always about getting the whole team together and having dinner or having a few beers. I always acted like I never had a bad day at the rink, other than a few times when I wasn't playing for suspension reasons.

PATRICE BERGERON
Bruins teammate

Shawn was humble. The DNA of a hockey player is you try to do your thing, and be your best, but be humble about it. But he sometimes forgot that he had that wealth of experience, and he had been around the game for a long time. He spent that time in the American Hockey League, and then he got the chance to win the Cup with Anaheim. He had that experience that some of us didn't have.

It started with Z, who always treated everyone with such respect. I might have been the opposite at times, when I would wonder why some young guy was getting off the bus first, or getting into the food line first, and probably wasn't shy about saying so. But Z would always say, "No rookies; we don't *have* rookies."

I saw it reported that Dougie Hamilton might have wanted out of Boston because he thought Z was too hard on him, and that is unfortunate and I have a hard time believing it, because I can promise you I would have been *much* harder. I'm a firm believer that if you've done a very hard job for a very long time at the highest levels, you've earned certain privileges. That's the same in *every* walk of life. If you're a cop, or you work in a steel factory, there is such a thing as seniority. Maybe I'm just from a different era.

In the minors, when we got off the bus, everyone pitched in and helped unload the bus. If you were a young player on the team, you better be unpacking two or three. Everyone was trying to help the trainers out, and young guys should want to do even more. If you're a young guy, you haven't earned the right to those privileges yet. I remember getting asked one time, "How long am I a first-year guy here?" And I just said, "Until you're a second-year guy. How hard is that to f—ing figure out?"

Z treats everyone with so much dignity and respect and always wants to help make his teammates even better every single day. Z is a straight-shooter. He's very disciplined and he has his ways, but he makes everyone around him better for that. Everyone is cut a little differently, and people relate to other people and other situations differently, but the leadership on the Bruins always started with him, and followed right on through people like Patrice and David and others. They would *never* allow someone to come into our room and not feel welcome.

ZDENO CHARA
Bruins teammate, captain

Let me put it this way. I have to say Shawn was the best guy in that role I ever played with. He was not the biggest guy, and he was not the strongest guy, but he had the balls of steel. He would always fight the biggest guys and the strongest guys. And he would hold his own. He really did such an amazing job for us. It was not just going out there and doing it. But he always did it at the right times and in the right place. He would make the most positive impact on our team. And you know, besides all of that, he was super tough and he was super skilled. He knew how to throw the punch. He didn't need a big wind-up. He would throw these really short, powerful punches. He also did a tremendous amount of work away from the rink. He took classes to make sure that whatever he did he could be best at it.

We were rounding into shape. We were coming together as a team, and we were getting ready to roll into the Stanley Cup playoffs.

CHAPTER 10

THE MERLOT LINE

WE USED TO JOKE THAT it didn't matter what people called us; we thought we were the checking line, not the fourth line. Look, I know we *were* the fourth line, but we felt like we had earned enough respect and rights, being that we played against the other teams' top lines. We probably felt that the "fourth line" moniker was a little degrading and diminished what our role really was.

The "Merlot Line" came about because of the practice sweaters we wore (maroon) more than a perceived lack of respect that a fourth-line title gave you. Claude called us the "Burgundy Line," but we felt we were more of a merlot, so I think that's how the name came about.

It actually started with Greg Campbell, Brad Marchand, and me. We started with that trio the first game in preseason in Belfast. Daniel Paille was on a different line at that point. Marchy played with us for the first 20 or so games, and he ended up buying merlot crushed-velvet jackets that we all wore sometimes on the road. But then Marchy started coming into his own, and he was having such a good start to the season that he got promoted up to play with Patrice Bergeron and Mark Recchi. When Brad moved up, Claude just slid Piezy down with Soupy and me.

MARK RECCHI
Bruins teammate

They had such great chemistry as a group. They were so reliable and they brought so much energy to the team. Greg Campbell was a great competitor up the middle, Danny Paille could fly, and Thorty was a smart player with a physical presence to him. They brought an identity to our team. We had a lot of great players, but I don't think we could have won the Cup without those guys. Claude Julien could play them against any top line. As a group we watched the Cup clincher against Vancouver not long ago, and they're out there against the Sedins, they're out there against Ryan Kesler. Claude had no problems playing those three guys against anyone.

I know what Rex said about us being crucial to winning the Cup, and we certainly liked to think that was true. Well, I don't know about, "We don't win the Cup without them," but we definitely took great pride in being able to play against the other team's top line.

MILAN LUCIC
Bruins teammate

Shawn and I weren't playing together on a line anymore by the 2010–11 season, but we definitely don't win the Cup that year without the play of the Merlot Line. They started the season with Marchy on that line, but Campbell had a career year with 13 goals, and Thorty had a career year with 10 goals and 10 assists. When Marchy moved up to play with Bergy, Dan Paille moved onto that line and fit just like a glove. They gave us energy, leadership, penalty killing, but they were also on the ice for a lot of important defensive zone draws. They made us a well-rounded team and took a lot of pressure off of other guys. I agree with Rexie—we don't win without them.

Where I got lucky was that Piezy and Soupy were probably third-line players on almost any other team, and I was fortunate enough to play with them. I was obviously a fourth-line guy. We used to joke that if I got promoted to the first line, then the first line just became the fourth line. It actually happened a couple of times. I think I got promoted to play with Krech and Blake Wheeler one time, so the guys said that instead of me being promoted that those two guys got *demoted* to the fourth line!

But my linemates had been third-line players on the teams they came from and would have been third line or higher on many other teams. It meant we played meaningful minutes against other teams' best players.

DANIEL PAILLE
Bruins teammate

During the playoffs we got the responsibility to play against the top lines and try to get our top units some rest. It was so important as the playoffs went along that we accepted that challenge and wanted that responsibility. We had such a confidence level as a line that we thrived under those conditions, because we wanted so badly to contribute. We were an energy line, and there were times we felt we had to provide a jump to our team. We provided a spark by making a big play, making a big hit or taking a hit, and stepping up physically when we needed to. We wanted to embrace that, and we wanted to show everyone that we weren't just a fourth line.

Danny was *so* underrated! He got us out of so many situations because of his speed, work ethic, and tenacity. Remember, he was a former first-round pick—20th overall by Buffalo in 2002—and he had a rocket of a shot on him. He didn't score as many goals as you would think with that shot, but he could skate like the wind and he was a very good body checker when we were playing physically against teams. He was probably the fastest guy on the team.

We just complemented each other very well. Soupy took some of the burden off me as far as the physicality was concerned, and Piezy could just rescue you when you needed him. I could literally just ice the puck, and I knew that Danny was going to beat the other team to the puck. I could just flip it into the neutral zone, and I knew those two guys were going to be in a battle for possession. We had plays where Piezy would play right wing and I would play leftwing, on purpose. When the puck was rimmed around, I could protect it and I could just shoot it off the glass on the far side in the first and third period. I would just shoot it right at his head and he would just skate into it and almost have a breakaway every time.

And you know what is *really* underrated? No one ever talks about how often Danny would sacrifice himself and his body for the team. He blocked almost 150 shots for us when he was playing for the Bruins. I think some other guys got a little more notoriety for giving themselves up, especially the guys back on the blue line, but Danny blocked a lot of shots and he blocked them well. He got a lot of scoring opportunities out of them too. If he had converted on half or more of the breakaways he had, I probably would have been a 30-point guy, and he probably would have been a 30-goal scorer. I did end up with 10 goals and 10 assists that year, which was a good year for me. It unfortunately wasn't a contract year.

And of course, Bruins fans will always remember Soupy for that one shift and blocking that one shot. We were playing the Pittsburgh Penguins in Game 3 of the Eastern Conference Finals in 2013, and Soupy laid out to block a shot from Evgeni Malkin. Unfortunately, the shot broke his leg, but we couldn't get control of the puck to clear the zone. They said he played almost a full minute after breaking his fibula until we could finally clear the zone and he could get to the bench. It didn't surprise me a bit, knowing his mental fortitude and how he approaches things. Look, he's a tough guy!

DANIEL PAILLE
Bruins teammate

I'm sure people don't remember, but I was out on the ice with Gregory during "The Shift." The thing I want people to know is that he was willing to put his body on the line for the good of the team. He sacrificed himself and his health for what was good for the team and for a win. I was in the middle of it, so it was hard to remember what was happening, but I've seen replays.

Look, most guys would stay down, and Gregory just kept going. We certainly didn't know that his leg was broken, although you had suspicions, but he just fought through it. There's a tremendous level of respect there from those who witnessed that and understood what kind of pain he was playing through. He's like Shawn in that respect. They both bring a certain respect from everyone for their commitment and willingness to do whatever it takes to get the job done. I often think how fortunate I was to play with both of those guys.

I've heard some people say the last shift the Merlot Line played marked the end of the Big Bad Bruins, and I think there's some truth to that. When we lost to Montreal, I played about eight minutes in that game and I think I was on the ice for a goal-against in that first period. But the optics of where the league was going and the differences between us and the Canadiens kind of stood out to people. They were the smaller, more skilled team, and I kind of felt like the writing was on the wall for our line and our style of play.

The Kings ended up winning that year, in 2014, and they played a style similar to ours. I feel like we perhaps could have handled them, and maybe even beat them, if we had gotten there. I used to joke with Willie Mitchell about it, and he admitted the Bruins were really built like a team from the Western Conference. I mean, look at the Blues' win against the Bruins in the 2019 Stanley Cup Final.

I'm still a big believer that you need a lot of skill, but I want skill that's willing to pay the price to win a game. I always felt like you needed a blend of skill and physicality. The year we won the Cup, I only had 14 fighting majors—certainly not a lot. There were years in the minors where I was having 35 or 40 fights in a season, and I had somewhere around 400 in my career. There were a couple of years in Boston where I had 20.

TRENT YAWNEY
Head coach, Norfolk Admirals and Chicago Blackhawks

I wasn't a bit surprised to see how Claude Julien used Shawn as part of that Merlot Line because I knew that ability was always there. You've got to earn the trust of the coach. You've got to be good on the boards whether you play five minutes or you play 15 minutes. We would tell Shawn to be good on the boards, get in on the forecheck. If there was a weakness to his game it would be that he didn't hammer guys finishing his checks. Shawn was like that when he fought—he finished you! But he could skate and he could intimidate people by getting in on the forecheck. The other guy would see that Shawn Thornton was coming, and they would suddenly release the puck as soon as possible and get the hell out of there!

But that Cup season was totally different. We were winning so much and I was playing so many meaningful minutes that I really made a conscious effort to *not* fight the guys who were playing one and two minutes a night, who were there for one sole purpose. I remember being challenged one night, and I can't remember who it was, but he really wanted to go. I was on the other side of the ice, and he's saying, "Hey, let's get them off right now!" And I remember saying to the opponent I was lined up against, "Why would I fight him right now? I've got 14 more minutes played than he does, and he's probably playing one shift while I'm playing against the top line." The guy I was lined up with actually said to me, "Yeah, I'm with you, bud."

And at that point in my career I think I had earned a certain respect. I had always given a fight to get one and I always tried to be respectful. I always had a lot of respect for the guys who did that. But that year, playing with that line, late in a game if we were up by a goal and I was playing meaningful minutes, I might not have fought just to fight.

And we had other guys too. Soupy, Quaider, Johnny Boychuk, Ference, Z, Looch, Kells—we had guys who fought a lot more that year. I wasn't relied upon to do it as much as I had been in the past. It was a real team effort that year.

We didn't have normal "year-end" interviews that season—it was a little hectic after winning the Cup. We were at Fenway Park with the Cup, and when we were done we went back to the Garden and did exit interviews. I don't know that I've ever had an exit interview that lasted any longer than a minute and a half. They're all the same—"You did your job. We wish you had scored some more goals. Thanks for being a great leader. We're not worried about you being in shape. See you next year."

That's what you can say about the Merlot Line in 2011. We won our last game and we did our job.

CHAPTER 11

MY BUDDY TUUKKA

SOME PEOPLE MIGHT FIND my friendship with Tuukka Rask a little weird. You know, the Oshawa tough guy and the Finnish goaltender. But people have to realize that Tuuks is just a good f—ing dude!

I first got to know Tuukka during training camp, and we hit it off right away. Then he was called up a couple of times when Manny Fernandez got hurt as Tim Thomas' backup. Shane Hnidy, P.J. Axelsson, Jeremy Reich, Milan Lucic, and I would take it upon ourselves to make sure we invited him out to dinner. We had a really tight team.

Tuuks was just a 20-year-old kid who was coming in to play backup for a few games. He was just happy to be in the league, and he wasn't afraid to go out and have a beer with the boys the night before a game because he knew he wasn't playing anyway. He was up and down, back and forth from Providence a lot. As one of the older guys, and with the leadership group we had, we embraced younger guys coming in, and Tuuks was one of them.

When I played in Norfolk, I lived with Lasse Kukkonen, so I got to really know a Finnish guy for the first time. For some reason, I just seemed to relate to Finnish people. I think they're amazing. Tuuks had played with Lasse on Finnish National Teams, so we had a bit of a connection beforehand. That's how our friendship started.

Then Tuuks became our starter. He and I have a lot of the same interests. We both love golf, we both like beer, we both love a good meal, and neither of us loves the spotlight. I know that seems contrarian, considering what we do, but we would both prefer to sit in the back of the restaurant and just enjoy our meal.

The guy people see now—the laid-back and mellow Tuuks—is a bit different from when he started. He's mellowed out as he's grown older, as we all do. The Providence YouTube sensation of him snapping and firing stuff all over the ice is him too. That passion is what makes him so great. He genuinely *hates* to lose. He's learned how to calm how he reacts to losses over the years, but internally it still chews him up to lose.

But we all mature. Back in the day, I would lose a fight and I would be firing water bottles all over the place. Later in my career, if I would lose a fight, I would just think, *All right. I'll get him next time.* You're still angry inside, but you learn how to compartmentalize it a bit more. Then when you need to use that feeling as fire you bring it back out, and Tuuks learned that. He's a competitive guy. But he's also not Tuukka Rask, arguably the greatest goalie in franchise history or one of the best goalies in the world—he's just Tuukka from Tampere, Finland. It wouldn't matter if he made a billion dollars or four dollars, he's the same person he's always been. I like to think I'm the same way, and that's probably why we hit it off so well.

One of our best mutual friends is Tommy McInerney, my boxing coach. Now, Tuukka's never boxed a day in his life, but Tommy is over at Tuukka's house almost every other day, and he was at our house every other day when I played in Boston. Tommy is a boxing coach and an electrician from Dedham, and those guys always hit it off too. Tuukka is a guy who enjoys going over to Ironsides in Charlestown and hanging out with Zack, who worked at and owned that place, more than he enjoys the ritzy dinners we might have out on the road. Tuuks is as blue-collar as they come.

TOMMY McINERNEY
Shawn's boxing coach and friend
I know people find their friendship a little strange, but Shawn and Tuukka just really get along. Tuukka is really chill and laid-back, when he's *off* the ice, and Shawn is actually the same way. When you think about Shawn's role on the ice—high-energy and physical—you would think he would be different off the ice, but he's the same as Tuukka. He's also one of the nicest guys around. He and Tuukka just get along, they never have any problems with each other, and they seem to have the same mentality. Both guys also have a good read on when to crank things up and when not to do it. They don't make stupid decisions. And both guys don't beat around the bush. They say what's on their mind, when they want to say it.

I've always been baffled by the way Tuukka is misunderstood by Bruins fans. I think they just expect him to be someone other than who he is. I think some fans expected him to be this superstar who sets himself above everyone else, but he's just not. He's really good at stopping pucks, but that's not what defines him. The game doesn't define him; his family does. How he treats other people and his friendships define him. The game has given him a lot of great things, and he never takes them for granted, but he's Tuukka because he's Tuukka, not because he plays hockey.

That goes back to when he left the playoff bubble in Toronto in 2020 during the pandemic. He has three young kids, and as he said, he had a daughter who needed help. He's a competitive guy and he wants to win, and he's an *amazing* teammate, but nothing means more to him than his family. And that is as it should be. Core values mean more than anything to him, and his family is the basis for those core values.

Tuukka's teammates were completely fine with what he did in Toronto, and I'm a former teammate who was more than fine with what he did. I said it then and I'll say it now—if I was in the same situation Tuukka was, I *would have left too!*

I'm a very outgoing person. I think I put myself out there and I'm out in the community and involved with groups and charities as much as anyone. But you can't find a picture of my kids anywhere. It's not my place to make my kids public figures just because I am. When they grow up, that will be *their* decision. Professional life is professional life, but *family is family.* I don't think Tuukka owed anyone any explanation for his decision. That's his call, obviously, but he should never have to explain anything involving his family. It's A-OK to *not* tell anyone about what happened with his daughter. That's nobody's f—ing business!

He made a decision, and he said it was based on his family, and that should be enough. The world should accept that we all have families, and they are more important than public opinion about what your decision is and how and why you made it.

My wife has been out to dinner with me when fans have wanted to chat or get a picture or an autograph. Erin has *no* desire to be a part of that world. She doesn't want to have photos out there and be a public person. And that's fine with me. It has nothing to do with who Erin is—it doesn't mean that she isn't a confident and accomplished woman. She just doesn't care if no one knows who she is, and that's her decision. I respect it. I'm just trying to say it's okay to keep your business and family sides completely separate.

The other thing people don't know about Tuuks is that he's freaking hilarious. I probably wouldn't hang out with him if he wasn't funny, but he's a *really* funny guy. He gets along with everyone and everyone loves him.

I'll give you an example. We went to Toronto and Tuukka met my two *idiot* buddies. One is a Newfie and the other is from Sudbury—Hubie and Crispy. A year after that, Tuukka was texting Hubie and Crispy and saying, "Hey, I'm coming into town. What are you guys doing for dinner tonight?" He's only met them through me, and they're not his teammates, but he tells me, "Hey, they're good guys. I like my teammates and I like to hang out with them, but I just wanted to hang out with Hubie and Crispy for the night."

We both lived in Charlestown. We just hit it off. We're both just basic blue-collar guys. It doesn't matter how much money we make, or whatever stage we're on, we just don't change. Then we bought the damned boat!

Tuukka had a place down on the water in Charlestown, and we lived just five minutes away up the hill. We used to hang out in that area a lot. We were out with equipment manager Keith Robinson for the year-end party after we lost to the Washington Capitals. We might have had one too many. Keito said he was getting a new boat for his place up in New Hampshire and was selling his old boat. We asked him how much, and he told us a price, and we just said, "F—k it! We'll buy it!"

The next day we were going in to clean out our lockers and do exit interviews. Tuuks and I each brought a check and gave it to Keito. Much later, I went home at a rather early hour in the morning, perhaps fairly inebriated, and told my wife I had bought a boat. She basically just said, "Shut up, you idiot, and go to sleep!"

A week and a half later, the boat was in the marina and Tuuks texted me, "I'm on the boat! Wanna come see it?" I was in the car with my wife, and I told her Tuuks was on the boat and asked her if she wanted to go see it. She said, "I thought you were kidding! You didn't really buy a boat, did you?" It probably was as mad as I've ever seen her.

Neither of us had kids at the time. We just thought we would buy it, drive it, float around on it, and drink beers on it, with a captain obviously. We got a good deal on it! We took it out every now and then, but we didn't use it as much as we should have, looking back on it. When we did use it, we had a good time. We rented a captain every once in a while, and took it up to Manchester to see friends, or over to Quincy. But it's not a lie when people tell you that the best two days of owning a boat are the day you buy it and the day you sell it.

ERIN THORNTON
Shawn's wife

Oh, don't even start about the boat! You know who I blame for the boat? I blame Brittany Lucic for this! We all went for drinks one night in Charlestown, and Brittany was the one ordering the pitchers of margaritas. She got them to dump an entire bottle of tequila into two pitchers. After that, suddenly we owned a boat!

Shawn says, "I grew up on boats." He grew up on a rowboat with an outboard motor on it! Growing up on a boat and owning a boat are two different things. We never made it from Point A to Point B without a siren going off or something going wrong.

One day, we were on our way back from Hull—and I don't even know how we made it that far to begin with—and Shawn grounds the boat and breaks off both motors!

Tuukka was the worst boat owner because he never really used it. And Shawn was the worst boat owner because he did! The best time for either one was when it was tied up outside Tuukka's place.

As I said, Tuuks is *very* competitive. It seemed like every time we played the New York Rangers, the Swedish/Finnish rivalry with Henrik Lundqvist got him going. You could feel it kick in for Tuukka when we were playing against them. Tuukka didn't dislike him; he just really wanted to beat him. I would love to see Tuuks' numbers against The King in those years when Henrik was considered one of the best goalies in the world. Tuukka took it to another level, because it was almost personal for him. It was like he was thinking, "He gets all the fame and all the glory, and he plays in New York, but screw him! I'm gonna own him tonight!"

When the story of Tuukka's Bruins career finally gets written—this year, next year, or five years from now—it's unfortunate how that story may go. Unless he wins a Cup in the next couple of years, the narrative will probably be "the greatest goalie to never win one." Unfortunately, that's what it probably will be.

In my opinion, the story should be that he was the greatest goaltender the organization has ever had, and he's an even better person. The last time I was in Boston, I went to his house and all of his teammates were there. He's a beloved teammate and a great friend.

CHAPTER 12

HIGHLIGHT

WHEN YOU DO WHAT I DO FOR A LIVING, the highlight reel is probably filled with surviving fights with some of the league's heavyweights. It usually doesn't involve shorthanded penalty shots. But suddenly it did, for one night in January 2012.

We were playing the Winnipeg Jets. Earlier in the night, I got stripped of the puck by Chris Thorburn, and after Dennis Seidenberg ("Seids") hooked him on the breakaway, he got a penalty shot. Luckily for me, Tuuks stopped him, but I knew it was my mistake that caused the breakaway, and my teammates had to pick me up.

Later in the game, I got called for a phantom check to the head penalty. Referee Greg Kimmerly even admitted to me later that he had messed up the call and he apologized. Mistakes happen, but Greg was a veteran ref, so I gave him the benefit of the doubt. We killed off my penalty and I came out of the box, probably playing guilty, just flying by my standards anyway, and I was in all alone on a shorthanded breakaway. I got hooked and suddenly I get a penalty shot.

My mom would probably tell you that I was always pretty good on penalty shots or shootouts. I had never had a chance to actually do one in the NHL, but I was actually better at them than most people would expect.

The surprise on my team wasn't that I could score on a penalty shot, it was that I actually *could get* a penalty shot! We would have competitions on the team all the time at the end of practice, and my teammates wouldn't think, *Oh, s—t, Thorty is an embarrassment!* I had the chance to work on that shot all the time in practice against one of the best goaltenders in the league. I used the same move in practice all the time, until Tuukka figured out what I was doing, and then it stopped working. So when they gave me the penalty shot, I skated down to Tuukka and asked, "Should I try it?"

TUUKKA RASK
Bruins teammate

I remember he skated toward me in the goal and gave me a little bit of a wink, like, "Should I do it?" I knew what he meant, and I said to him, "Hell yes, you should do it!" Then he went down and dangled the goalie out of the net and scored the goal. I was so pumped for him! And I remember everyone else on the bench was so excited for him too.

There I was against Ondrej Pavelec, just me and him. I wasn't going to try a backhand, leg-lift toe-drag in practice; I was going to try it in a real game, against real competition, and in a jam-packed TD Garden. You would think I knew what I was doing, and I had my first and only penalty-shot goal in the NHL.

SHANE HNIDY
Bruins teammate

My first year in the broadcast booth, I was with the Winnipeg Jets, and we were making our first visit to Boston. Wouldn't you know it, Thorty gets a penalty shot. I said on the air, "No one knows or expects this, but he's probably going to do a backhand, leg-kick, toe-drag thing and go shelf." No goalie in the league is going to expect Thorty to do that unless they've been in a practice with him. But that allowed me to have my Tony Romo moment and correctly predict exactly what he was going to do.

Seids told the press after the game, "I don't know how many guys can do that. I would have ended up in the corner if I tried that." David Krejci said, "It was a pretty sick move. I've seen him do it before so I knew he had that. He's got some balls and he scored a goal that was a really big goal. All the players on the bench were very excited and happy for him." Nathan Horton added, "Shawn has more skill than a lot of guys. He's pretty good with the puck, and you've seen the penalty shot. Not too many guys can do that."

MILAN LUCIC
Bruins teammate

Before he pulled off the backhand toe-drag, I was kind of expecting it. We were on the bench calling what he was going to do. I was much more surprised that he even *got* a penalty shot. We had seen that move in practice a bunch of times, and he had pulled it off. Hell, I've played almost 1,000 games in the NHL, and I've never even had a penalty shot! Those are hard to get. But that's one of the things that is underrated about him. Thorty had skills, and he could play!

Now, I hadn't taken a penalty shot in front of actual people since the Max Milk Midget Tournament. Oh, and I won that shootout competition, by the way, and I have the belt buckle to prove it. I'm also sure that Scott Gomez either doesn't remember or doesn't want to admit it, but I beat him in that competition. But I had never had a penalty shot in the pros...not in the AHL or in the NHL. I was nervous. I guess I'm all alone out there in front of everyone when I fight, but I'm much more nervous with my hands scoring goals than I am with the other stuff. So later in the period, I got to do that "other stuff."

ZDENO CHARA
Bruins teammate, captain

Shawn was a very skilled player. Many times in practices he would be throwing these perfect sauce passes in the air. These passes would be seven feet in the air and they would land on the guys' blades, like perfectly. I recall there was one game when he had two goals in, like, three shifts, and everybody was trying so hard to set him up for that third one, so he could get the hat trick, but it didn't happen. We were all trying, and we wanted it so much for him. I think even Claude began to realize, like, "I have to play him now, like every other shift." But as soon as Shawn had two goals he was almost too humble to score the third one. I think Shawn felt that if he scored a third one there was gonna be too much attention on him, and that's not what he wanted.

Jets defenseman Mark Stuart is a good friend of mine. He was with us in Boston before being traded to Winnipeg, and we became very tight. But tight doesn't mean much when you're in battle in a real game.

Stewie cleared me out in front of the net after the whistle and I took exception to it. He's a good friend of mine, and a character guy. I was sad to see him leave here, but I also knew he was the type of guy who would be pushing back and would stand up for himself. I certainly wasn't going to let him take liberties with me so I pushed back, and we went. I would still buy him a beer after the game if I saw him. No hard feelings. All business.

It's funny how the game goes. At that point in the season I had been in 10 fights and six of them had been against former teammates—Travis Moen, Jim Vandermeer, Krys Barch, Zenon Konopka, and Stewie. When you've been around the game as long as I had, it was bound to happen from time to time.

It was a night to remember. Outside of championship games, it was one of my favorite moments ever. And a chance to show that—sometimes—even tough guys get a chance to shine.

CHAPTER 13

AN IDENTITY IS BORN

OUR TEAM HAD REALLY BEGUN TO GEL BY FEBRUARY 2011, and from that West Coast trip just before the trade deadline, we felt like we had the makings of something special. We had brought in Chris Kelly, Rich Peverley, and Tomas Kaberle in three separate trades between February 15 and 18, and while the trades might not have made much of an impression on the fans, they sure did with us. From the time they joined us on the trip, all three just fit in perfectly. It was like they had been playing with us all season long.

We knew the team was pretty good, and we also knew who we would open the playoffs against—the Montreal Canadiens. I know how special the Bruins-Canadiens rivalry is for hockey fans in both countries, and I can promise you, it's the same for guys wearing the uniforms. We don't like them, and I'm pretty sure they don't like us, and that makes the hockey even more special.

We felt we had a pretty tough hockey team and could play any style of game the opponent wanted. We had skill guys who could skate and score, and we had tough guys who actually liked it when the game got a little rougher. But you have to go back to the game on February 3 to find the moment this Bruins team became a group no one wanted to play against.

We were hosting the Dallas Stars, and Bruins fans still talk about it. Before the game, Gregory Campbell told us he had issues with Steve Ott of the Stars, and he wanted to settle things right off the bat. It had all started back in 2009, when Ott had taken a pretty good run at Gregory when he was playing for the Florida Panthers. Ott hit Greg when he wasn't looking with a pretty vicious charge, and Soupy never forgot. Of course, it was a complete coincidence that after seeing Ott was starting for the Stars, Claude Julien decided to start our line—Gregory, Daniel Paille, and me.

When the puck hit the ice for the opening faceoff, so did the sticks and gloves for Campbell and Ott. It was a pretty spirited bout until Ott got a couple of shots in, and a forearm to the face opened Soupy up a little bit.

As we lined up to get things restarted after that fight, Krys Barch and I started talking. Now, I had known Barchy pretty well from our minor league days, and I always respected his game and his toughness. I actually taught him how to fight when we were teammates in Norfolk. He asked me if I wanted to get them off, and I kind of understood where he was coming from. He felt he had to do something after the Ott and Campbell thing, and he did it the right way. I was happy to oblige him.

Barchy and I had squared off a few times before, and he was certainly game, but as the fight drifted from the right side of the faceoff circle to the opposite side of the ice, by the Bruins bench, I caught him with about three or four really good rights. He didn't go down, and he acted like he wanted to continue, but I could see I had messed up his eye a bit, and I asked the linesmen to step in and break things up. I certainly didn't want to hurt him any more than he already was. He didn't play again that night and was out of the lineup for a while.

But we weren't done yet. As the teams lined up for the third faceoff in the first three seconds, Brian Sutherby felt like he had to respond, so he challenged Adam McQuaid. Sutherby got a couple of pretty good shots in, but Adam acted like he didn't even feel them—because he probably didn't. Four straight shots right to the chin put Sutherby down and that was it. Three fights in four seconds to start the game and a little different feel to our team identity.

Let me just add this—I knew what I was doing in situations like that, and I knew what my job was. I signed up for it and was happy to do it. But there is something about putting your body on the line for your team and then giving up a goal right after that can really let the wind out of your sails. It always pissed me off when, right after a big fight (or in this case, three of them), your team gives up a soft goal or you take a bad offensive zone penalty. So when Milan Lucic scored for us, just 35 seconds into that first period, you felt like it was all worth it. Patrice Bergeron scored maybe a minute later to make it 2–0, and the Garden went absolutely bonkers! For all intents and purposes, the Stars were done. We won the game 6–3. A side note—the Stars' goalie that night was former Bruins goaltender and current NESN analyst Andrew Raycroft. He gave up those two goals on the first two shots he faced and was pulled. It certainly wasn't his fault, but he didn't make the stops, and we won. I even added a goal, from Paille and Chara, in that first period.

DANIEL PAILLE
Bruins teammate

I remember that game against Dallas. There was such intensity, but also such a feeling of camaraderie and team spirit. Within the first minute or so, there were three fights going on. First Soupy is fighting Steve Ott, followed by Thorty fighting Krys Barch, and then Adam McQuaid is battling Brian Sutherby. Just five minutes after that, Andrew Ference is fighting Adam Burish. That's when I think we realized that playing Claude's system was important, but it was even more important that everyone was playing for each other. You really wanted to battle for the guy beside you. From that point on, it went through the entire season.

That set things up for what happened just six days later when we hosted the Canadiens at the Garden. We had a pretty good idea we might meet these guys in the playoffs, and we were definitely trying to send a message to Montreal.

You had an idea of what the night was going to be like when Milan Lucic and goaltender Carey Price drew matching roughing minors to end the first period, but we were just getting started. When the night was done, there had been six fights and 187 minutes in penalties.

In the second period, things escalated. Brad Marchand started things off with a charging penalty, while Zdeno Chara and Brian Gionta drew matching roughing minors. But the highlight was a real-life, honest-to-goodness goalie fight. Tim Thomas and Carey Price both left their creases and went at it. Now, look; neither is gonna be considered a good fighter—not many goalies are. But they were willing and gave it a go. As I said, we went into the game thinking we had to send a message.

Late in the third period, David Krejci and Benoit Pouliot squared off. Now, Krech is one of our skill players, and he should probably never be fighting. He had a broken wrist the previous season, maybe killing our chances against the Flyers in the playoffs. But it sent a huge message to our team that he was willing to step up and at least try. To give you an idea of how unusual it is for him to fight, he went nine years before his next regular season fight. Lucic and P.K. Subban got misconducts, and McQuaid and Roman Hamrlik got fighting majors and game misconducts. We won the game 8–6, and the message had been delivered. But it was also a game in which Tim Thomas and David Krejci had fighting majors and I didn't. Funny game.

We had another regular season incident to get through against the Canadiens that also helped set the scene for the playoff series still to come.

We traveled to the Bell Centre on March 8 for our first game against Montreal since that epic in Boston. It was a pretty uneventful game, and we actually didn't even play that well, losing 4–1. We actually lost four of the six games against the Canadiens that season.

It was late in the second period and Max Pacioretty was flying up the wing, near the Canadiens bench, when Zdeno Chara delivered a check that got the police involved—well, Montreal fans and authorities wanted them to get involved.

Big Z is the biggest and strongest man I've ever seen play the game. Sometimes, I'm not sure he realizes just how strong he is. He smashed into Pacioretty by the Bruins bench, running him into the side glass at the end of the bench and knocking him out cold. Pacioretty was taken off the ice on a stretcher, and Zdeno received a five-minute interference major and a game misconduct, but the Bell Centre fans wanted blood. When they didn't get it on the ice—and I mean, who wants to try to deliver that against Z anyway—they looked for other ways.

Chara was not suspended by the NHL. But I can also tell you that Z felt just awful that Max was hurt on the play. He certainly had no intention of injuring anyone. The NHL decided it was simply a hard hit that is part of our high-speed sport, but people in Quebec were not willing to let it sit there. Quebec's director of criminal and penal prosecutions, Louis Dionne, asked police to begin a criminal investigation into the hit. Max, to his credit, even said he did not want to see the legal system involved. Ultimately nothing further came from the incident, other than even more heat on the Bruins-Canadiens rivalry and alterations to NHL arenas. The league instituted a change and rounded glass partitions were installed in every arena, a positive out of a terribly unfortunate incident.

It was simply more fuel on the fire for the Bruins and Canadiens. We met one final time in the regular season, but it was a very tame 7–0 win for us. We were playing out the regular season and getting ready for the Stanley Cup playoffs. That playoff run would, of course, have to begin against the Montreal Canadiens.

CHAPTER 14

THE RUN TO THE CUP

I WISH I HAD AN ANSWER for how that first-round series against the Montreal Canadiens started. We ended the regular season on a high note, we were healthy, and we certainly felt like we were ready, but looking back I guess we weren't.

I remember we really had a tough time with the Canadiens during the year too. The last game of the regular season against them, we really wanted to make a statement and we shellacked them 7–0. There was a bit of a donnybrook at the end of the game. We certainly realized in the room there was a good chance we would end up playing them in the playoffs, and we wanted to send a message.

We started the series in our building and ended up going down the first two games. Some message, huh? We were probably all a little shocked, but thankfully the team we had was not afraid of a little adversity. We had enough character in the room that we embraced it a little bit. We certainly didn't *want* to be down two games to none, but we were and we had to figure out what we were going to do in their building, a tough place to play a game.

We started the series on April 14 at TD Garden, and Brian Gionta scored both goals for Montreal in its 2–0 win. We outshot them 31–20, but Carey Price is an elite goalie and certainly played like it that night. And remember that donnybrook in the regular season? Nothing here.

There were only seven minor penalties called, which for a Bruins-Canadiens playoff series is pretty unemotional.

Two days later we played Game 2, and it didn't go any better. Price got the better of us, but at least there was a *little* more emotion. Shane Hnidy fought with James Wisniewski, my old teammate. The bottom line was that Montreal was heading back to the Bell Centre with a 2–0 series lead, and we had to figure things out—fast.

The beauty of playoff hockey is you *usually* play every other day (more about that in a minute), so you get to climb right back in the saddle. We were certainly ready to do that in Montreal. The Canadiens outshot us 36–25, and it was the first time in the series that Tim Thomas got the best of Price. I just remember that the Canadiens played well, but Timmy stood on his head and we were alive.

Because of the extra day between games, and because our management knew what the media scrutiny is like in the playoffs in Montreal, they decided to take us out of town for a day. We hopped on the buses and headed for Lake Placid to practice at the Herb Brooks Arena. Now, first, I'm Canadian, and second, I like Montreal, so I would just as soon have stayed in the city for the extra day. I'm sure the field trip meant a lot to the American guys on the team, but the 1980 USA Olympic hockey goal medal doesn't mean as much to us guys from north of the border. It was fine. It was practice and when they say go, we go.

Game 4 was almost sleepy by Boston-Montreal standards. There were only three minor penalties called, but what the game lacked in PIMs it more than made up for in goals scored. We were down 1–0 after one but Michael Ryder, Andrew Ference, and Patrice Bergeron scored in the second. Then Mike Cammalleri and Andrei Kostitsyn also scored for Montreal, and we were tied going into the third.

P.K. Subban can certainly shoot the puck, and his power play goal gave Montreal the lead, but Chris Kelly tied things up later, and we headed for overtime. Michael Ryder scored his second of the game just two minutes into overtime, and we had what we needed—a tied series heading back to Boston for Game 5.

For the second straight game, we needed extra time to settle things—but a lot more of it. After two scoreless periods, Brad Marchand and Jeff Halpern traded goals in the third period, and we were going into overtime. Actually, this one took two overtime periods to get a winner. The legend of Nathan Horton began when he scored at 9:03 of the second overtime to give us a 2–1 win and a 3–2 series lead. We outshot them 51–45 and both goalies were great, but we were ready to go back to Montreal to try and finish things off.

Now, either the Bell Centre and Montreal Canadiens management weren't very confident in their hockey team, or something fell through the cracks, because our schedule for Games 6 and 7 got shuffled because Lady Gaga had the building booked. I'm probably better equipped to understand the idea of revenue streams now than I was back then. That meant we had an extra day in between Games 5 and 6, then had to play on back-to-back nights in two different cities, which is certainly unusual and not ideal. Canadiens greats of the past had to be rolling over in their graves at the thought!

Game 6 was really frustrating. We could only get one goal past Price, but Cammalleri and Gionta scored for Montreal. Gionta's goal came with a two-man advantage after Bergy shot the puck over the glass. They were already on the power play because Milan Lucic got a boarding major and game misconduct. At least the emotion was picking up. Not only did we get to go back to Boston for Game 7, but we got to do it the very next night.

The rivalry with Montreal is certainly different than any other rivalry we have in the NHL, so in that respect a playoff Game 7 has to be different too. But Game 7 in the playoffs is still Game 7. It's win and move on or lose and go home. That doesn't change.

Going into the game, you're nervous because you don't want to be done. You feel like you have a lot more hockey to give, and you don't want to squander that opportunity. Montreal is always heightened, no matter when you play that team. There is a palpable energy that you feel anytime you play the Canadiens.

I've looked back and saw that I took an elbowing minor in the first period of that game, but I can't honestly tell you anything about it. I'm sure I hit someone, and it looked a little high, but I can promise I wasn't happy about it either. *Deserve* has nothing to do with it—I'm sure I didn't like the call.

When we got to overtime it just made sense that Nathan Horton was the guy who scored the game-winner. He was so low-key and so laid-back that he didn't want anyone to even know he scored the game-winner. It's kind of hard to hide from a Game 7 overtime game-winner against the Canadiens, but Horty would have if he could have.

When the game was on the line, we had a couple of guys on our team who you wanted to have the puck on their stick, and Horty was definitely one of those guys. Now, he would never admit that, but he was one of those guys. He knew that he wanted the puck, but he would never tell you he wanted it.

I know the baseball stats people say there is no such thing as "clutch," but I do believe in it, and Nathan Horton was a guy who was clutch. I would never put words into his mouth, but I think Horty flourished with us because we had guys in Boston who were already superstars in the NHL, so he didn't have to be the face of the franchise. He definitely wanted to win the games, but it was always for the team and not for the notoriety.

We had Z, we had Timmy Thomas, we had Bergy—we had *All-Stars!* Looch was already a folk hero by that point. That meant Horty could be happy just being a complementary piece. He didn't have the pressure of carrying the team and being its best player. He just didn't have that with us. Even if he *was* the best player, he didn't have that pressure on our team.

We moved on to the second round and we got to play the Philadelphia Flyers. After the complete meltdown from the year before, it seemed fitting that we got to play them again. We had been holding onto that for a year. It had been a motivating factor for us the entire season. We definitely wanted to make a statement. We were certainly aware that making a statement to them was secondary to just moving a step closer to our ultimate goal, which was to win a Cup. We were a pretty even-keeled team in that regard, but we definitely hadn't forgotten what had happened the year before.

We won Game 1 7–3, and you would like to think a message was sent, but we were well-versed in how tough a town Philly is and how tough the Flyers were to play against. It's the culture and DNA of their organization. We certainly didn't take anything for granted, that's for sure.

Sean O'Donnell was with the Flyers that season. He and I like to think we see and play the game a lot alike. I played with him in Anaheim, and he's a really smart hockey player. He might be quiet, as far as speaking up is concerned, but he's a natural leader. I like OD a lot—I've got a lot of time for OD. But that doesn't mean I didn't want to beat him.

In Game 2, Horty set up David Krejci for the overtime game winner. Krech was a guy who took his game to another level when we got to the playoffs, and he always has. The year before he was leading the league in playoff scoring going into that Flyers series, and I would like to think things may have been different if he hadn't gotten hurt.

He's another guy from our team who was quiet and understated and didn't want the notoriety. In fact, he wasn't given as much as he deserved. But when the game elevated, Krech had another level, and he *really* wanted to win.

We won those first two games in Philly and came home for Game 3. Z scored 30 seconds into the first period, and as crazy as the Garden was, the bench *didn't* go ballistic because we had been down that road. The year before we were up 3–0 in the first period of Game 7 against the Flyers and going nuts on the bench. We learned that while it was exciting, and you celebrate, you then refocus and get ready for the next shift and the next play. We knew it could be taken away from us as quickly as we earned it.

Z had two goals and an assist in that 5–1 win in Game 3. I think people who only remember Z from his last couple of years in Boston forget what an offensive force he was earlier in his career and certainly in that playoff run. He was always a penalty-killer and shutdown defenseman type of player, but he had serious offensive skills too.

In my years with the Bruins, Z was quarterbacking our power play. He was a superstar. Z was a 6'9", 270-pound monster who scored 10 to 20 goals a year from the back end. He got a lot of points on the power play, and a lot of our offense ran through him. I didn't see as much of him after I left the Bruins, but that's the way I always remember him. We were trying to set him up to shoot, because he had the hardest shot in the National Hockey League.

So we moved onto Game 4 to try and clinch the thing. Marchy scored an empty-net goal to make it 4–1, and Philly pulled its goalie again because it had nothing to lose. I played a little more than 3:30 in the game, and I think only Sheriff played less, but Claude put me out on the ice at the end of the game.

I can't tell you how I felt about that in the moment, so it probably didn't mean very much to me. But I will also say that I always truly believed that whatever was best for the team was fine by me. I went on the record in the next series when Claude took me out of the lineup as saying that we're always team guys, but when you're trying to win a Cup it's even more important. Ice time doesn't f—ing matter, goals don't matter, plus-minus doesn't matter—*nothing* matters except winning.

You do whatever it takes. There's no bitching, there's no saying, "Oh, he threw me on the ice for the last minute or so when the game was decided!" All you want to say is, "We won." End of story. I can't stress this enough—nothing else matters! I was just happy to pad my time-on-ice numbers, and I even picked up an apple on Paille's empty-netter.

We won the first two rounds, and Timmy was good for us in goal. We didn't give up a ton of goals, and we were moving onto the Eastern Conference Finals, but it was after that Flyers series that Timmy's game went to an even higher level. It certainly helped Tank that the second round was a little bit of an easier series for him, from a goaltending perspective. But at that point, Timmy wasn't the centerpiece of the conversation. We won the game, and he was good, but we weren't relying on him to steal games or a series for us at that point.

I know it didn't end the way Timmy might have wanted it to at the end of his Boston career, and he caught some flak from the fans after skipping the visit to the White House. But Tank and I were friends, we hung out. We got along great. Now, was he a little different? Yeah. Did we have different opinions? Sure, but that doesn't mean you don't like a guy. I've had different opinions about many things than a lot of people. But Timmy and I got along great, and I've got a Stanley Cup ring in large part because of what he did for our team.

Did I go to Burger King for a double burger with him after practice some days? Yeah, I did. But some days we didn't go, probably because I was trying to mix in a salad here and there. We went out for beers on the road, and he was in our dinner crew sometimes. There were times when he wanted to be and other times when he didn't.

We moved on to face the Tampa Bay Lightning, a very skilled team, and I had prepared myself for what I thought could happen. It wasn't really much of a conversation with Claude. I prepare for every game the same way, whether I'm playing 12 minutes or sitting in the press box. I played a little over eight minutes in Game 1, and we lost 5–2. In Game 2, I played less than five minutes and we won the game 6–5.

Bergeron was dinged up and didn't play in either of the first two games in Tampa, but he was ready to come back into the lineup in Game 3 back in Boston. Tyler Seguin went into the lineup when Bergy went down and he *went off!* He had two points in Game 1 and came back with four more points in Game 2. So when Bergy was ready to go in Game 3, Claude stayed with the hot hand and I was the one who got scratched. I just wasn't a necessary piece to the puzzle at that time. I completely understood. You can't pull a kid out of the lineup who had six points in two games.

161

I was able to keep a positive attitude despite being pulled, in part because I had been through it before. I had been in and out of the lineup a lot during my career. I was aware that winning the Cup was all that matters. No one remembers, at the end of the day, if you were in for Game 2 or you were in for Game 5. I certainly want to have an impact anytime I'm in the lineup, but it really doesn't matter. All that matters is winning. Segs was the right choice at the time. Bergy was coming back, and I knew what was coming. You never like sitting out, but it didn't shock me, nor was I negative about it.

I was scratched for that Game 3 in Tampa, and I was sitting in the dressing room looking around. In fact, I think NESN reporter Naoko Funayama brought it to my attention: the Lightning had pictures all over the place from their Cup win in 2004. They still had guys on their team who were part of that championship. We really didn't have anything around our room or even in the rink of our franchise history. We're an Original Six team, so we should have as much history to look back on as anyone. Why didn't we look at reminders every day of who we were and how we got there?

Later that night, Shane Hnidy and I were having beers and talking about it. We had both been scratched, so we stayed up a little later and had a few more beers. First, we went to Claude and told him our idea and he was all for it. We grabbed equipment manager Keith Robinson and asked him what was available. We said our team needed reminders of what we were trying to accomplish. We were getting close, and we needed reminders of what was at stake.

Keito spoke to a sports memorabilia guy and ended up grabbing a bunch of photos. We had Bobby Orr drinking beer out of the Cup! We needed photos of guys bleeding in the Stanley Cup Final back in the '70s. We needed to be reminded of the magnitude of what we were trying to accomplish here. We probably should have thought about it earlier, but Keito got it done by the time we got back to Boston. Everywhere we looked we wanted to be reminded about what was at stake.

I'm certainly not saying that was the reason we won the Cup, but it turned out to be a positive that came out of me being able to sit back and hot stove what was going on and what we could add to the team. We wanted to help, even though we weren't on the ice at that point.

The team thought it was pretty cool when we got back to Boston and all the stuff was hanging there. Rex, assistant coach Doug Jarvis, and I brought our Stanley Cup rings in and laid them out for guys to look at. When you've been there and won your last game of the year, you have a better idea of what is involved. It's a whole different world. You're a Stanley Cup champion for the rest of your life. It doesn't go away, and they can never take that away from you. I know the team understood the message, and they seemed to really like it.

We got to Game 7 for a chance to go to the Stanley Cup Final. There were no penalties, but it was tough, hard-nosed, hard-hitting hockey. It was an incredible game to watch, even if I couldn't play in it. Sheriff and I watched the game from the ninth floor of TD Garden. It's tough to watch when you're not out there, but you just want to win. But from that vantage point we had a great view of how the winning goal transpired.

The play that produced the only goal of the game was a play we drew up ahead of time. We were having a hard time getting through their forecheck with our normal system. We came up with a way to beat it. Rex, Z, Bergy, Ference, Looch, Krejci, myself—we all just sat around and brainstormed on how to get through their forecheck.

We were doing a lot of quick ups, and their 1-4 system always had a defenseman sitting back there waiting to break things up. If you couldn't hit the zone with a lot of speed, it was hard to recover pucks. That was the beauty of the Tampa Bay system. The downside is that four guys are standing still in the neutral zone, so we had to find a way to take advantage of that.

We all had a hand in figuring out a way to break through, and Rex said, "This works. We're bringing everyone back, and we're going to attack and create two-on-ones through the neutral zone."

I remember watching it and seeing the play unfold. It was exactly the way we had drawn it up, and I remember thinking, *Holy f—k! It worked!* The guys on the team put it together, and the guys on the ice worked it to perfection. This isn't taking anything away from Claude or the assistant coaches. But this wasn't Claude drawing it up on the board; this was the boys saying, "Hey, let's communicate, let's work together. How do we figure this out?"

Seeing it come together, it almost looked like it happened in slow motion. When Krech's pass went across the crease and Horty put it into the net, you felt like this was why we had a great team. We figured it out together, then we executed. Was Claude okay with it? Well, we won, so I would say yes.

We moved onto the Stanley Cup Final to face the Vancouver Canucks. They had won the President's Trophy with the best record in the NHL, and they were a prohibitive favorite and probably should have been. But that didn't matter to us. We didn't see Vancouver all that much during the season, and maybe we didn't know what we didn't know, but we definitely didn't think we were underdogs. We were also not intimidated in the least! We thought we were just as good a team as them, if not better. I wouldn't say we were cocky, but we were confident.

It was a weird series, in a way. When we played in Vancouver, the Canucks had their way with us at times. Then we came home for Games 3 and 4, and we won 8–1 and 4–0.

But then we went to Vancouver for Game 5.

The Canucks beat us 1–0 to take a 3–2 series lead, but the task just didn't feel as daunting. We were certainly not worrying about playing in Vancouver for Game 7 if we were lucky enough to get there. They won the game, but it was anybody's to win. Max Lapierre scored the only goal of the game about five minutes into the third, but we outshot them and played right with them. We just thought, let's get some rest, go back home, and take care of business.

Game 1 was in Vancouver, and Raffi Torres scored the only goal of the game with 19 seconds left in the third. I was sitting in the stands, so I didn't have much to do with what happened in the game, but I wasn't okay with it at all. Sheriff and I were watching, and we didn't like what was happening in that game or in Game 2 either.

We are both very proud guys and fairly tough individuals, so it was hard to watch the Canucks taking physical liberties with our guys. I wasn't in the room right after the game; the last thing guys want is to see you in your suit after the game when they're still pissed about what just happened. By the time you get back to the hotel, everyone calms down a little bit. You have a meal, maybe have a beer, and you can look at things with a little perspective. By that time, you can chalk it up to losing just one game and get ready to move on to the next. You hang onto it until midnight, then you let it go and get ready for practice the next day.

We moved on to Game 2, where we lost in overtime. Alex Burrows scored the first goal, assisted on a third-period goal, and then got the winner in overtime. I didn't realize until I looked back on it how impactful he was in that game. Of course, I still wasn't down on the ice, so I was frustrated from up above. But he was the entire package—the mouthiness, the way he plays, the finger wagging, the biting incident with Bergy. He's an agitator and that's his job. But he also produced in Game 2. With everything else he had been doing, it was just like rubbing salt into the wound for sure.

Maybe there was a little part of me that was thinking I should have been in the lineup before that. I had even talked to Claude about it and pleaded my case. I told Claude that I knew Segs was a much more skilled player than I would ever be, but I also brought up the fact that being in the Final was something unto itself. I told him I was one of three guys on the entire team who had been there, and I tried to make the argument for going back into the lineup for Game 1.

It didn't happen, but after what happened in the first two games of the series, that conversation maybe helped steer things in the direction they went in Game 3. The tone of those first two games probably helped make my case. I'm certainly not taking anything away from Segs—he's a way better player—but somebody brought up our actual record when I played in the playoffs (13–5) as opposed to when I sat out (3–4). That was certainly favorable for me.

We got on the plane back to Boston, and Claude told me to be ready because I was going back into the lineup. After what happened in those first two games, I kind of expected it. I was excited. I started getting ready because it was like Game 1 of the Stanley Cup Final for me. It had been a couple of weeks since I had been in the lineup so I was just jumping at the chance. I felt like I was ready to be shot out of a cannon—except I'm not fast enough to be a cannon.

You grow up your whole life dreaming about playing in the Stanley Cup Final. You role-play and pretend on the street that you're playing for the Cup. That feeling you have as a little kid never leaves you. By that time I was 34 years old and had already played for and helped win a Cup. But you wait your whole life for it, and that leads to a heightened sense of excitement. Obviously I wanted to set the tone, if I could, when I got in the game.

My teammates will all tell you that I take it very personally if people are trying to take advantage of someone on my team. I wanted to send a message to the Canucks in Game 3 that what they did in the first two games would no longer be acceptable.

I got on the ice for the second or third shift, and I was very fortunate that I was put in a position to finish a check, I think against either Burrows or Maxim Lapierre. I finished the check and the crowd at the Garden was going nuts. I was back in the lineup and there was real energy in the building. Our whole line played with a lot of energy, finishing checks and really trying to push the pace. It worked out really well, especially because we won the game 8–1.

Claude was simply rolling out four lines, so our line didn't necessarily have a specific matchup assignment. But the Canucks were often doubling up their top line, so if that meant we were going on the ice when the Sedin twins were, then so be it. Even if they didn't double up, they went first line, second line, third line, then back to the first. Sometimes that meant we were out there against their top line, but Claude was fine with that. He had confidence that if Alain Vigneault sent the Sedins over the boards, it didn't matter because our line was still going.

PATRICE BERGERON
Bruins teammate

I agree with Rexie 100 percent—we probably don't win the Cup without the play of the Merlot Line. Just think about Game 7 against Vancouver. The Merlot Line kind of set the tone, and we scored some goals later, but early on the Canucks were coming at us and there wasn't much room out there. They had some chances and Timmy made some great saves, but I thought the Merlot Line had a couple of shifts where they sustained some pressure and got momentum for us. They helped turn things around early on. But that entire playoff run, they were *so* important to our team. They were popular with the fans, and for good reason.

Of course, I also got kicked out of that game, so that limited how many minutes I could play. Now, you'll probably be surprised to hear that I didn't think it was warranted. There were some scrums and I think I just grabbed Ryan Kesler, but it was some five-on-five clutching and grabbing. I was out there trying to make sure things *didn't* get out of hand, but I got kicked out and I think things *did* get out of hand after that. I'm not sure that stuff would have happened if they let me stay in the lineup. But for some referees there is a certain stigma around certain players like myself. Sometimes the ref thinks it's better to get you out of the game than let you stay, and I think that was the case here. But

I also thought it was counterproductive. I got a roughing minor and a misconduct, but things certainly didn't get any smoother with me gone. Look at the penalties called after I left—boarding, roughing, fighting, slashing, slashing, charging.

That was the game where Aaron Rome knocked Nathan Horton out for the rest of the playoffs with a vicious head shot at the blue line. We certainly didn't like the hit or the result of the hit. Horty was knocked unconscious and had to be stretchered off the ice. It certainly didn't look good for Horty. You hope for the best, but we kind of had a feeling it was bad. I also guess it speaks to our depth that we could lose a key player like him and have a guy like Tyler Seguin to put into the lineup. I don't know how the team looks if Horty got hurt and we didn't have a player like 19-year-old Segs to step right in. If someone like me had to go into the lineup, and now there are two of me, it's a totally different structure.

I can tell you we decided it was going to be Vancouver's last big hit of the game. We had a thing during the playoffs where we gave this old-school Starter jacket to our player of the game, and after the game that jacket was hanging in Horty's stall.

Then Looch and Rex were chirping the Canucks and putting their fingers near players' mouths, daring them to bite them like Burrows did in Vancouver. Claude didn't like that one bit and even called the guys out on it after the game.

Things were starting to get a bit out of hand. Dennis Seidenberg even fought with Kesler, and Seids almost never fought. Timmy Thomas just obliterated Henrik Sedin with a check in front of our net. We were certainly ready to go for Game 3 back home, but you could make the case that the Aaron Rome cheap shot against Nathan Horton turned the series completely around.

It was after that Game 5 win for Vancouver that Roberto Luongo said some things he came to regret. Now, I got to know Lou real well when I went to play for the Panthers, and he's really a great guy. At that time I really didn't know him at all. We had a job to do, and if that meant blowing up what Lou said and trying to get him off his game, then so be it. He made some comments that were probably taken out of context, and we decided we would try and jump on that and feed of it, as you should. I heard then-Patriots safety Rodney Harrison once admit he would make stuff up to get mad at the other team, and I agree with Rodney 100 percent.

Brad Marchand once said in an interview, "People say they'll do whatever it takes to win, but really, will you?" I will. I will do whatever it takes to win.

ROBERTO LUONGO
Vancouver Canucks goalie
I've been pumping Tim Thomas' tires ever since the series started, and I haven't heard one nice thing he had to say about me, so that's the way it is.

TIM THOMAS
Boston Bruins goalie
I guess I didn't realize it was my job to pump his tires. I guess I have to apologize for that. I'm the goaltender on the other side, and I stick with all the other goalies.

We did have to make three cross-continent trips during the series, and that means five six-hour plane rides. Actually there was a sixth trip, but it was after we won the Cup and we didn't give a damn about that one. Most of us would use the opportunity to catch up on some rest. Rex and I would sit together and shoot the breeze, telling stories. Usually Tomas Kaberle and Hnidy would come join us at some point. That meant a lot of storytelling and hanging out. We would also talk about the next game and what we thought would happen. It certainly wasn't very exciting stuff, just resting and getting ready.

There were some guys who would play cards, but I'm just not a gambler. The way our plane was configured there were about 20 player seats in the middle of the plane, then the galley area where the flight attendants would be working, and behind that there were four seats with a table in between and the same across the aisle. Rex and I sat in that area, in the aft of the plane, for every trip. He isn't much of a gambler either. We didn't play cards, but that was always going on in that center section.

We weren't superstitious, but we would always sit in the same seats for every flight. Rex and I had some tenure, as did Z and Bergy. So we just sat in the seats we liked, and the guys would be respectful of that. If the seat wasn't available, or we had a different plane, that wouldn't have affected me one bit. Like I said, I wasn't superstitious; I just liked where I sat. Of course, I'll also admit that if we sat in the very back there were no eyeballs on us, and we could sneak a little wine onto the plane too. It's a lot easier to have a couple of glasses of wine in the back of the plane.

Sharing a glass of wine with Rex was also one of the highlights of my career. He called me the night before Game 7 in Vancouver and asked me to come up to his room in the hotel. He had a great bottle of wine and he wanted me to have a glass with him. He also wanted to tell me that the next night was going to be his last game. He didn't want to make a big deal out of it, and he wasn't going to tell the team, but he wanted me to know this was going to be the end of the road for him. It was a helluva road, too—a road that would end at the Hall of Fame.

MARK RECCHI
Bruins teammate

Shawn and I had become very close over the years. We would sit in the back of the plane together. We had become that close that I wanted to share with him that this was going to be my last game. I wanted to have a glass of wine with a really good friend, look out over the Pacific Ocean, sit and talk, and get ready for Game 7. I'm so glad he came up to my room. It was an awesome night for me, the night before my last game.

We got to go back to Vancouver for Game 7 and the chance to play for the Cup. I know the TV showed Horty with the bottle of water from the melted TD Garden ice, spreading it on the ice at the Rogers Arena, but I certainly had no idea he was doing that. I honestly don't know if I found out about it after the game or three weeks later.

I'm a little bit of a different breed. Before games I go into my own little cocoon. I get ready on my own, mentally, and I wasn't really aware of anything else going on around me. I know that assistant coach Geoff Ward gave a speech before the game. I sort of remember that it was really good, but I couldn't tell you the first thing about what he said. My preparation was a little different. I had headphones on a lot, and I guess I was like a boxer before a big fight.

I know we won Game 7 4–0, but for me I felt it was over with about two or three minutes left to play. We had been bitten a few times in the past, certainly by Philadelphia the year before, but this just felt different. With about two or three minutes left in the game I just knew we had it. We were too good and too dialed in to let this one slip away. That allowed me the chance to really drink things in over those last few minutes.

The horn sounded and we just went streaming onto the ice and up to Timmy, like every other team does. Then you just go around screaming

171

and hugging everyone you see. I was lucky too because my dad made the trip and he was down on the ice with us after the game. He was interviewed on Canadian TV by Scott Oake. That just made it even more special. He still brags about it to this day! I'm still not sure how Scott knew that was my dad, but knowing my dad he probably went right up to Scott and introduced himself.

ERIN THORNTON
Shawn's wife

The Bruins flew all the wives out to Vancouver for Game 7 of the Stanley Cup Final. I was the only one who had been through it before, when we were in Anaheim. I was trying to tell the girls to enjoy it before because I knew that if they won, none of us was going to be allowed down on the ice. Basically we were all waiting down under the stands. I told them that if things went well, just sit in the stands and take pictures. That was the best part, to just sit and take it all in. It's not really about us anyway; it's about them. It was just so much fun to watch—I'm getting kind of emotional just thinking about it again.

I'm not a bit surprised that Erin was coaching up the wives as the game came to an end. I have no doubt in my mind. But if you've never been through it, you would have no way of knowing what's going to happen. She did have that experience. I didn't know at the time she was helping the other wives, but it makes total sense.

We flew back to Boston, and when we got to the Garden, Z was taking the Cup someplace. Being captain has its privileges. But Tuuks and I wanted to thank the people who work behind the scenes. So we grabbed the Prince of Wales Trophy—the Eastern Conference Trophy that no player wants to touch—and headed for the Bruins offices. We also made sure we brought some beers.

Tuukka and I then spent some time drinking beers with the office staff, celebrating with them and thanking them for all they do for us. They seemed a little surprised when we came barging into the office, but I also think they appreciated the thought. We get all the credit and all the glory, but all of them work so hard, especially when the team is on a Cup run.

MATT CHMURA
Vice president, Boston Bruins

As soon as we touched down in Boston, Cam Neely and I had to go right to the mayor's office to start making plans for the Duck Boat Parade. After meeting there for a while, I headed back to the team offices and there were Shawn and Tuukka, taking the Prince of Wales Trophy around the office and having a beer with everyone. That was just the type of guys they were. They couldn't bring the Stanley Cup around, so they did the best they could. I think that Prince of Wales Trophy actually ended up staying in my office for quite a while after that. The Cup was the trophy that mattered.

We certainly celebrated the Cup win like you're supposed to. The guys had a great time in the city of Boston on Friday night, while Erin and I were privately celebrating our wedding anniversary. Then on Saturday we all gathered in the back parking lot of TD Garden for the start of the Duck Boat Parade. Marchy did a horrible job singing "Black and Yellow" from the staging and even got Bergy to sing along.

When I arrived at the Garden, I was expecting there would be two or maybe three rows of fans on the sidewalks to watch the parade. Partly because we had a perfect Saturday in June, but mainly because hockey fans had waited 39 years for this day, the crowd was *way* beyond anything I could have ever imagined. Every sidewalk, for every inch of the parade, was packed with people from the curb barriers all the way back to whatever building was behind them. Boston Police said at the time it was the largest championship parade in the city's history. Estimates were that well over 1 million people came out to celebrate with us. Trust me when I tell you that Boston is a sports town first and foremost, but it is definitely a hockey town!

After the parade, we made our way to McGreevy's, owned by my friend Ken Casey of Dropkick Murphys, then it was off to a team celebration at Foxwoods Resort and Casino in Ledyard, Connecticut.

A lot was written about our bar tab to celebrate our win. The entire team went to Shrine at Foxwoods. Someone took a picture of the bar tab, and it got a lot of attention and sort of went viral after it was posted. I guess a bar tab of $156,679.74 will get some attention. It also got skewed a little bit by the $100,000 bottle of Ace of Spades Midas. I mean there were only six of those bottles in existence at the time. Other parts of the tab crack me up—like 67 bottles of Fiji water at $4.00 a bottle.

Now do you want the less exciting truth of the story? We actually paid less than $156,679.74—a lot less. I was friends with Ed and Joe Kane and Randy Greenstein of Big Night Entertainment Group. They added to their ever-growing restaurant and entertainment empire when they opened Shrine. I gave them a call to ask if they could help me set up a night for the team. We wanted to get outside of Boston for a few hours, and Ed and Joe invited us to Foxwoods. They set up a team bowling event, then blocked off an entire floor of Shrine just for us for the night.

They had heard about Mark Cuban buying a huge bottle of Ace of Spades Midas for the Dallas Mavericks when they won the NBA Championship the week before, and they were determined to find a bigger one for us. The $100,000 bottle was twice as big as Cuban's. At the end of the night, they just asked us to take care of the staff, and they comped everything else on the tab. A bartender took a photo of the actual tab, and posted it somewhere and the story grew legs at that point. The amount was legit, but Ed and Joe took care of it. The guys put together the amount to take care of the staff, and the $24,869.80

came from us. We were happy to pay it. Hey, if you win Boston's first Stanley Cup in 39 years, you should do it up a little bit, and we did.

We spent the night at Foxwoods, and a bus picked us up the next day to take us to Fenway Park to participate in a mini Duck Boat Parade and ceremonies before the game. We may have actually lost a few soldiers who didn't quite make the trip with us back to Boston.

As I said earlier, I had become friends with then-Red Sox president Larry Lucchino and senior vice president Sarah McKenna over the years, when Erin and I spent a lot of nights in the summer watching baseball. In fact, Sarah is on the board of directors for my foundation. When we arrived at Fenway, Larry took me aside and said, "Shawn, I don't give a f—k if these guys drink out of the Cup before our game today! I want them to see what winning feels like and appreciate what the rewards are."

So after a Bloody Mary or two, we headed for the Red Sox clubhouse, and things got a little loud and rowdy down there. The Sox guys were so happy for us and crowded around us yelling, high-fiving, and getting a look at the Cup. We might have also taken Larry up on his offer and given guys the chance to get a drink from the Cup. Big Papi held the Cup over his head just like Zdeno Chara had done just a few nights before.

The camaraderie and spirit between the Boston sports teams was unbelievable. Of course, there was a lot of winning going on and all four teams had titles during that run. But each team supported all of the other teams. I became great friends with a number of players on the other teams and have relationships with them even today. When the Red Sox or Patriots came to our arena after winning championships, we were as excited for them as they were for themselves. And when we brought the Cup to other teams' venues, those guys were just as fired up for us.

In the fall, the Patriots invited us to bring the Stanley Cup to a game at Gillette Stadium, and we were happy to oblige. When we first arrived, we met with Bill Belichick and he spoke to our team for a few minutes even though he had his own game to worry about. We had the

Cup at midfield for the coin toss, then the Patriots arranged for a suite for us to watch the game.

Unfortunately we had a game ourselves the next night, so there was no drinking for us, but we had fun being there. At one point, my friend Kevin Youkilis of the Red Sox texted me and asked me where we were watching the game. He said he was also at the game and invited Tuukka and me to come by and say hello.

We headed out and had arrived at the suite number that Kevin had given us when two stadium security guys swooped in. They apologetically said, "Mr. Thornton and Mr. Rask, we know who you guys are, and we're very sorry, but this is the one suite we are not allowed to let you enter."

I mentioned to them that Youk had invited us, and they went inside to have Kevin come out and escort us in.

What I didn't know was that Youk was dating a young lady named Julie Brady. In fact, they were married a year or so later in New York. If that name sounds familiar, it should, especially to Patriots fans. Julie is Tom Brady's sister, and the suite we were barred from entering was Tom's suite. When we got in, the entire Brady family was there watching the game, including Tom's wife, Gisele Bündchen.

I'm not sure Gisele knew who we were aside from the pregame ceremonies, but she could not have been more friendly and generous. She welcomed us into the suite just like we were long-lost Brady brothers.

That was kind of the end of our Stanley Cup celebration, but it was a memorable one—and certainly one I will *never* forget.

CHAPTER 15

MY DAY(S) WITH
THE CUP

THE STORY IS THAT the New Jersey Devils began the tradition of allowing every person involved in winning a Stanley Cup championship their own personal day with the Cup back in 1995. The NHL also began assigning a "Keeper of the Cup" to accompany the trophy on every visit, in every country, that year as well. Whoever thought up the idea, my hat is off to them, because I think it's one of the great traditions in sports. As a kid growing up in Canada, you always dream of winning a Stanley Cup, but I never dreamed I would ever be spending a day with the Cup—let alone multiple days.

The league puts together a master schedule of Cup visits almost as soon as the championship is awarded, and you generally get about a month's notice before the Cup comes to your house. Not long after we won in Anaheim, and I got notice of my date, I started to seek out advice from people I trusted about how to handle this. I think it was Brad May who gave me the best advice.

I told Brad I was going to bring it to my old arena, where I first wanted to have my picture on the wall and was told it would never happen. I was going to have an open session, and if people donated money to charity they could have their picture taken with the Cup. I thought that would have been awesome. But Brad told me, "Thorty, you've worked your whole life for this opportunity and you've got to find a way to thread the needle between giving people the chance to enjoy it with you and not having it being taken away from you for the day." It was great advice, and I think I found a way to maintain a pretty good balance with it. As Brad said, "If you do a big thing downtown with 10,000 people, but 10,200 show up, it's the 200 who don't get their moment with the Cup who you will hear about the most, no matter how hard you try to do the right thing."

Mike Bolt was the Keeper of the Cup for every visit I ever had with it, starting with the Anaheim win. He was coming to my house from Kent Huskins' house in Colbert, Ontario. He got to our place at about 8:30 or 9:00 in the morning, and Erin immediately put a Canadian Bloody Mary, better known as a Caesar, in his hand to make him feel at home.

You're kind of planning for this day your whole life, but now here it was finally coming to fruition. Mike came to our house in Oshawa, and we had a gathering planned with people we knew, friends and neighbors, to come over for an hour or so to take pictures with the Cup.

From that point, I jumped in my car and went to visit my grandmother. She had been suffering from Parkinson's and she was in an assisted living facility at that point. She was still very sharp, but she was suffering physically and used a wheelchair. She could still talk; she just couldn't move the way she used to. She knew what was going on and she was smiling from ear to ear. I'm pretty sure she had been bragging to everyone that her grandson had won the Cup, so all of her fellow residents had a pretty good idea we were coming.

We spent the next couple of hours there and one of my favorite Cup moments *ever*, to this day, was when I helped my grandmother hold the Cup over her head. She was a big part of my hockey life, and she was my biggest fan, so I was happy I could give something back to her. Then we took the Cup into the common space there at the facility. First we took a big group photo, then I made sure everyone who wanted to could get their own individual photo with the Cup.

When we left there we went to grab a bite and stopped at a few local establishments near the house so our friends could get a look. After a couple of stops, we went out to Wyndance Golf Club, which had recently opened nearby. I think I had nine foursomes of friends and family who were going to play, and I played a hole of golf with each foursome. Whoever was closest to the pin on the hole got to use the Stanley Cup as their ball marker.

After golf, we went back to the house and changed and got ready for dinner. We went to The Keg Steakhouse in Oshawa for a quiet dinner with just close family. After dinner we went to a place called the Waltzing Weasel, a local watering hole that was a 10-minute walk from my house.

My friend Ashley owned the Waltzing Weasel and we put together 300 tickets that we sold for $10 each. If you wanted your own photo with the Cup, I think we charged $40, and every dollar went to the Parkinson's Foundation. That was my big shindig for my day with the Cup. Lionel Ingleton was there, as were people my dad worked with in the mills and friends I hadn't seen in a long time.

We tested the rim of the Cup first to make sure it would be okay, then we *did* make a margarita to serve out of it. A lot of people grabbed a straw and we all enjoyed a margarita out of the Stanley Cup.

At the end of the night, because both my new friend Mike Bolt and I were a little inebriated, we decided we had to play a game of rock-paper-scissors to see who had to carry the Cup out to the limo. Luckily I won the most important game of rock-paper-scissors I've ever played, so Mike had to carry the Cup. Both of us were nervous about delivering the Cup safely, but luckily Mike was able to pull it off. No harm, no foul.

Mike actually stayed at our place that night. Erin, our two dogs, and I slept with the Stanley Cup that night. The next morning, Mike had to go to Ric Jackman's place in Barrie, Ontario, which was about two hours away from my house. I actually woke Mike up, and while he was getting ready to leave, I took the Cup out back to hose it down and clean it up for the next stop. We delivered the package to the Holy Grail's carriage and Mike headed on down the road.

In 2011, there were a few of us who got the Cup for a couple of days. The others were Mark Recchi, Z, Timmy Thomas, and Andrew

Ference, I think, but Cam let me have it for an extra day because I was one of the only guys living in Boston in the off-season. He gave me the chance to have the Cup for a day in Boston, then to take it back home to Ontario for a day. I was very fortunate.

I was staying in Toronto, and the Cup was actually flying in from Tuukka's visit with it in Finland. It was scheduled to arrive in Toronto at about 9 PM that night, and I was scheduled to have it for the next day. Once again, my friend Mike Bolt called me and said, "It's coming in; do you want to have it the night before too?"

I set up a quiet dinner with only about 12 people invited. None of the people knew the Cup was coming, so they were having dinner with me for all the right reasons—because they were just great friends. We were having dinner at the top of the CN Tower and Mike brought the Cup there at about 9:30. I told my friends I would be right back and met Mike downstairs, then brought the Cup up to my group. My friends were *pleasantly surprised* that they were getting a special, personal night with the Cup.

We were staying at my friend Hubie's house. After dinner, my buddy Billy Hickey from Newfoundland, who is a musician, came over, and we just set the Cup up on the roof deck, had a few beers, and listened to our own private concert. I'll tell you about a little larger private concert later on.

The next morning we were going back to Oshawa to start the day at my parents' house. I explained to them that we had already had a day at home with the Cup after the Anaheim win, and I just wanted a simple, quiet group at their house to start the day. I told them we had taken care of everyone the first time, and that everyone who needed to see it had put their hands on the Cup and taken pictures with it in 2007. I said that we would grab Tim Hortons and then just invite the important people, like my grandparents, my sister, my nephew, my cousins, and a couple of close friends. I planned on a quiet breakfast at the house to start the day, then to go back into Toronto later in the day. My parents told me, "Yup, no problem!"

I got to the house that morning and there was a line on the sidewalk that stretched about 10 houses down the street. All of those people were waiting to get into my parents' house! Plans change, and I knew everyone there, so it wasn't like I was upset about it. I ended up taking pictures with everyone, and I spent a couple of hours there, which was fine.

We went from there to Erin's parents' house, which was much quieter. Some of Erin's family was there, and we were in her folks' backyard by their pool. A couple of my friends who didn't come to my parents' house were there with their kids, and we took pictures with all of them too.

Then we headed back to Toronto. Our actual plan was to go to my friend Rob's place, Bier Markt. We had a band booked and everything. But first, we stopped at the Flatiron Building, which is an iconic building in Toronto. It was a really cool-looking building with a patio out front. So we went there for a beer, and we were sitting on the patio with the Cup, and I remember people walking by saying, "Look at that a—hole with the fake Stanley Cup on the patio! What kind of idiot would do that?!" They didn't even realize they were looking at the actual Stanley Cup.

After we got changed and ready for the evening, we got ready to walk to Bier Markt, which was only about five minutes from my buddy Hubie's house. At that time, I learned to carry the Cup over my shoulder, which was the only way to get it from my house to there, because that damn thing is heavy! We walked the Cup down the street in Toronto and you would be surprised how many people didn't even notice. We had a crowd of about 20 friends with us, so maybe if people did notice what we were doing, they didn't dare say anything.

There were about 250 people at the party at Bier Markt, and a bunch of my friends made arrangements to come into the city. Guys like Dave Duerden and Jim McKenzie and a bunch of my childhood friends with their better halves all got hotel rooms downtown and everyone had a great time.

After we finished, we went back to Hubie's place again. Hubie gave Erin and me his room, so we had the master bedroom. Erin had gone to bed a little (maybe a lot) earlier than me, and a bunch of us sat on his roof deck again, drinking beer and listening to Bill Hickey playing songs from the Tragically Hip and others. And, yes, we were drinking from the Cup.

I went to bed very late and brought the Cup to bed with Erin and me. Mike had to take the Cup to wherever it was going the next day, but when he was ready to go, we were sound asleep. I know I brought it to bed with me and Erin, and I also know that when we woke up, the Cup wasn't there anymore. I guess Mike came to get it from us, and I'm going to assume he saw some things he shouldn't have seen! Mike admitted to me later that when he came to take the Cup from us, he made sure to go to the other side of the bed from where I was. If he was going to see something, he didn't want to see it from me!

Then, in September, I was given a second day with the Cup. It was just after the Deutsche Bank tournament in Norton, and I played in the Pro-Am with a guy named Brendan Steele. He is a huge Los Angeles Kings fan, and he was at the Anaheim Ducks game when we won it in 2007. We really hit it off, so when he was finished with the tournament he was going to fly out to the next stop on tour. I suggested we grab a bite to eat before he left, then casually just said, "Hey, do you want to go see the Stanley Cup?" It was at Andrew Ference's place the day before I was supposed to get it again. So we sort of crashed Andy's Cup party. Steelie and his caddie got to drink out of the Stanley Cup. We weren't there very long, because I didn't feel right crashing Andrew's party, but my golfing friend got to see the Cup.

The next day, Mike Bolt brought the Cup to our house early in the morning. We grabbed a coffee, and then we immediately took it to Ironsides. We didn't announce we were going there, but word travels fairly quickly in Charlestown. So we ended up being at Ironsides for about three hours.

We had rented a limo and we were doing the rounds. We had to stop at McCarthy Liquors. They've been at the bottom of Bunker Hill

Street for more than 100 years and Richie McCarthy became a pretty good friend when we lived there. Then we stopped at the Warren Tavern, followed by Old Sully's, which is no longer there. If you saw the Ben Affleck movie *The Town*, you saw Sully's.

Then we made a visit to Children's Hospital. We met Katie Devine there and spent the next two hours trying to visit every single kid we could with the Stanley Cup. It was *amazing* to see the smiles on those kids' faces, and I'm so happy we were able to spend time with them.

After Children's, my plan was for a photo op at Fenway Park. I think the Sox were actually on the road at the time, but is there a more iconic photo spot in Boston than on the Green Monster at Fenway Park? I always remembered the photos of Scott and Rob Niedermayer with that photo on top of a mountain. I don't live in the mountains, so in Toronto we took a picture on the top of CN Tower, and in Boston we took one on top of the Monster.

After our photos, we went down into the ticket offices at Fenway Park. The Red Sox people were always so great to us and some of those people working in the offices never get to see the light of day. We took the Cup down there and let everyone take pictures with it.

That was followed by a quick stop at Navy Yard Bistro in Charlestown for a very small dinner with a group of friends. Then it was time for the big shindig.

A month or so earlier, Ken Casey of Dropkick Murphys and I were talking and he just said, "Hey, when you have the Cup here, would you like us to play a couple of songs for you?" Of course, I jumped at the chance!

We put together our big party at The Royale downtown. I had about 200 people there, and I think the band had another 100 or so, and Dropkick Murphys were going to play a private concert for us. I literally thought they were going to play three to five songs, but they ended up playing for almost three hours!

It was an amazing experience. I remember being up on the balcony with my mom, my aunts, and Erin, and I knew everyone was there for the Cup, and not for me, but it was one of those life moments. How does it happen in my life that one of my favorite bands is rocking for three hours with my friends and family and I helped put it together? I don't know how to explain it, but it was just surreal.

But no sleeping with the Cup this time. After the concert, we went home and Mike went back to the hotel that night. It was a much quieter end to the festivities this time.

But I wasn't quite done with the Cup.

In 2018, the Florida Panthers played the Winnipeg Jets in Helsinki in the Global Series game. I accompanied our CEO, Matt Caldwell, to represent the Panthers. The NHL had the Cup over there in Finland, and my old friend Mike Bolt was there to chaperone. I think we spent a week in Finland, and I remember it was over Halloween. That put me in the doghouse a little bit, because it was the first real Halloween for my daughter Nora, and I wasn't there to experience it with her.

Mike helped me get out of the doghouse though. He told me he hadn't seen Erin in a few years, and he pointed out I didn't have kids when I won either Stanley Cup. He said when we landed in Miami, he was heading from the airport up to The World Golf Hall of Fame and asked if I wanted him to swing by the house. Are you kidding me?

He pulled out a map and showed me he was driving practically past where I live in Parkland. So Mike came by the house and we invited a few neighbors over to visit. I honestly don't think that many people even knew at that point that I played hockey, or understood what I did. I remember one neighbor was from Michigan, and I think his eyes almost popped out of his head when he saw the Stanley Cup sitting in our living room.

We were able to take pictures with the girls with the Cup. Ainsley actually fit inside the Cup at that time, and Erin, Nora, and I took pictures with her and the Stanley Cup in the backyard. It was pretty cool that I got to spend another couple of hours with it and my girls got proof that their Dad actually played on two teams that won it.

CHAPTER 16

THE LIST

Warming up with
the Blackhawks in 2005.

Tommy McInerney and me after training with friend and legendary boxing coach Freddie Roach.

Freddie wrapping my hands before one of the toughest training sessions I ever had.

Having a few words with the Blackhawks bench after taking a skate to the face. I ended up needing 40-plus stitches.

A dream come true, hoisting the Stanley Cup in my first full year in the NHL with Anaheim.

© Jim McIsaac/Getty Images

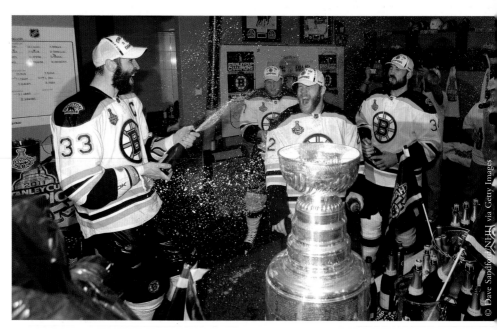

© Dave Sandford/NHLI via Getty Images

Celebrating in the locker room in Vancouver.

Hoisting my second career Stanley Cup.

© Bruce Bennett/Getty Images

Ryan Crisp and me enjoying a beverage on my first night with the Cup in Toronto.

The night of my Dropkick Murphys Cup party in Boston with Julian Edelman and Zoltan Mesko.

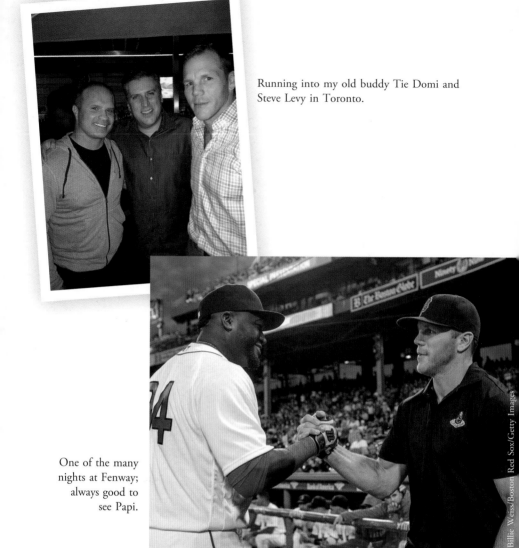

Running into my old buddy Tie Domi and Steve Levy in Toronto.

One of the many nights at Fenway; always good to see Papi.

© Billie Weiss/Boston Red Sox/Getty Images

One of the numerous occasions jumping on the Jimmy Fund telecast and supporting a great cause.

...oston Children's holds a special place in my heart and the Shawn Thornton Foundation continues to ...upport it annually. Check presentation with our friend Katie Devine.

The smile says it all. Bringing the Cup to my grandmother's home, where she was battling Parkinson's, was the greatest part of winning the first one in Anaheim.

...elping Nanny hoist the Holy ...rail. This moment for me was ...ven better than when I raised the ...up over my head.

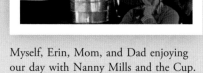

Myself, Erin, Mom, and Dad enjoying our day with Nanny Mills and the Cup.

Listening to Billy Hickey on my buddy Hubie's back deck in Toronto.

Support from Bruins fans in Florida the night I became the first player to play 600 NHL games after playing 600 in the AHL. I was the third player to accomplish 600/600.

Kenny Florian rocking my jersey before his UFC fight in Vancouver against Diego Nunes. We were playing the Canucks in the Final at the same time.

At my parents' house with mentor and former coach Lionel Ingleton.

At Ken Casey's golf tournament supporting the Claddagh Fund along with the great Bobby Orr.

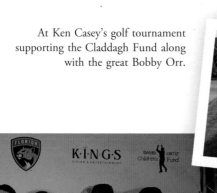

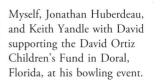

Myself, Jonathan Huberdeau, and Keith Yandle with David supporting the David Ortiz Children's Fund in Doral, Florida, at his bowling event.

ly amazing teammates sending me off into retirement after my last game.

Just catching up with my buddy Tuukks in warm-ups, chirping him about how many goals I was going to score that night.

I wanted to capture a picture in my gear with my daughter, Nora, while I was still playing. This was before one of our home games before I retired.

Presenting the Stanley Cup to the Stoneman Douglas hockey team after they won the state championship.

THE KIDS TELL ME everyone likes superlatives lists: favorite, least favorite, best, worst, hardest, easiest—well, you get the idea. So with that in mind, I thought we would take a swing at it and run through some highs and lows, best and worsts from my professional career. Let's kick things off with:

Favorite Place(s) to Play: I probably have different answers and different places for different reasons.

Toronto would be first, because I would get to see my family and friends from back home in Oshawa. I was also playing in the second generation of a building that I grew up idolizing and wanting to play in. When I was a kid it was Maple Leaf Gardens, but that got replaced by the ACC. Now it's the Scotiabank Arena, but it's all Toronto and it was cool just for that reason. It's home, and my parents got to watch me just 45 minutes from where I grew up.

As far as overall atmosphere is concerned, I would have to go with Montreal. I don't care what side of the table you're on; when you get in there with that huge arena and that crowd, it's hard not to get fired up. Montreal just has an energy that you can't replicate. That U2 song starts, the lights start blinking, and the crowd just goes nuts! The energy is like nothing else. It's 20,000 people and you can just feel it in your gut.

When you talk history, it's also hard to pass up Madison Square Garden. It was always cool to play there, but much better after they made their upgrades. I didn't always *love* playing there because often it was an afternoon game, they usually had tough guys, and the lights were terrible for the first few years I was in the league. The lights were yellow, and I always thought it made it harder to see.

Least Favorite Place(s) to Play: I may have more than one answer to this one too. Look, it's the NHL, so none of the arenas are terrible. There were certainly some places in the minor leagues that I hated playing in.

I'll start with Ottawa. I *hated* playing in Ottawa! The arena is in the middle of nowhere. It is four hours from my house, but I never liked playing there.

I certainly didn't like playing in Pittsburgh when the Penguins played in the Igloo. The new building is beautiful, but the Igloo was just *not* a fun place to go play.

I seemed to always play pretty well in Raleigh, but I can't say I enjoyed playing there very much. That might also be because I felt like I was scratched from the lineup half the time. It's a pretty sleepy area, and the building has all those basketball banners hanging up reminding you which sport they really care about down there.

You can even take the buildings out of the equation, and a lot of it has to do with the city you're visiting. I'm a big foodie, so a lot of my impressions have to do with the city and the restaurant scene.

Place to Have a Beer with a Friend: I'm going to leave Boston out of this for now, because that's probably a bit of a different list. Plus, there might be too many places to mention here.

I would say it happened most often in Toronto because a couple of my best friends live right downtown, but we switched up the bars all the time. For a long time my buddy Rob Medal had a place called The Beir Market, where I had a Cup party, but he sold it eventually.

Where to Go for a Fine Dining Experience: This one is pretty easy. I would go with Maison Publique in Montreal. That place is amazing.

The owner, Derek Dammann, is actually a big Bruins fan. Derek and I have a common friend in Jamie Bissonnette, who owns a bunch of restaurants in Boston. It looks like an Old English pub, but the food is amazing. Derek would usually say to me, "Do you want to see the menu, or do you want me to just cook for you?" He is one of the best chefs I've ever had the pleasure of being around. His food is just f—ing phenomenal! Every time I'm there, it's something different and every time it's perfect. The first time I was there he made me a steak, and I went online and bought his cookbook the very next day. Then I asked him to send me the secrets for any of the rubs he put on the steak. The next time I was there, he had just gotten a deer and he made venison ribeyes. Another time he had elk. It's just an amazing experience, soup to nuts. Derek just gets it.

Where to Spend a Day Off in the NHL: It probably always starts with a place I can golf. Arizona, Los Angeles, Anaheim—somewhere warm that allows me to play a golf course that is potentially in the top 100. And before you ask—no, I do *not* have an ace, and I'll thank you to not rub that in.

An Opponent I Liked Playing Against: I'll probably surprise some people here and say Eric Boulton.

We were very similar players and played junior hockey against each other for a lot of our younger years. We disliked each other extremely. Then when I roomed with Shane Hnidy in Boston, I found out he used to room with Bolts in Atlanta. We were having a beer one night and Shane said, "Thorty, I know you can't stand Bolts, but you're actually f—ing identical twins, and you would probably love him if you ever met him." I played another 10 years against Bolts, and we probably fought another dozen times. I got to know him, not well, but well enough that we could punch each other in the face for two minutes, and then go to the penalty box and talk about it afterward. He plays the game hard but he's very respectful. He rode that line extremely well and I don't think he ever crossed it. He chipped in when he could, and he's a better

191

skater than a lot of people give him credit for. I like Bolts. He did his job the hard way. He's the same size as me, and he had to fight the big boys but was never afraid of anyone.

I'll give you another name in the same category as Eric Boulton: Michael Rupp. I really appreciated the way he played. We had some real battles and I think he got the better of me in like 90 percent of our fights, but he played hard and he also did things the right way.

An Opponent I Didn't Like Playing Against: There are probably different guys for different reasons. There were some guys who were so skilled that I didn't want to be on the ice with them. Evgeni Malkin just absolutely undressed me in the neutral zone one time. He made me look like I played men's league and he played for the Russian National team—which he does!

I've been on the record talking about Alexei Emelin and how much I disliked the way he played the game.

But I was legitimately nervous playing against Derek Boogaard. He was a big, scary individual.

If You Were an NHL GM, Who Would Be Your First Pick in the Draft? If we are talking about players in their prime, I think I would have to go with Sidney Crosby. He simply makes everyone around him better all the time. I also think Patrice Bergeron is like that. But Sid just takes everything to another level.

Who Is the Best Player in the NHL Today? Well, I can tell you the most exciting player, without a doubt, is Connor McDavid. People should tune in to watch a game just because of him. It doesn't matter if you're an Oilers fan or a Bruins fan or a Panthers fan; he is that f—ing exciting! No one can control the puck the way he does at the speed he does, and then he seems to be able to turn his speed up to another level while doing things most players have to slow down to do. It looks like he's dangling, but he's gaining speed while doing it. He's remarkable, and he's fun to watch.

What Goalie Did You Feel You Owned? Listen, when you play like I did, it would be presumptuous of me to say I owned *any* goalie.

I probably had more goals against Cam Ward than I should have. And I probably scored more goals against Ondrej Pavelec than I should have when he was in Atlanta and Winnipeg. Pavelec gave up the only penalty-shot goal I ever scored in the NHL, but I seem to remember scoring other goals against him too.

Funniest Teammate You Ever Had: Keith Yandle was pretty funny. But P.J. Axelsson comes to mind first.

Teammate the Fans Least Understood: He was only in Boston for a short time, but I think Bruins fans didn't understand Tomas Kaberle. I knew him from Toronto and he was a first or second defenseman for the Leafs. He played as a No. 6 guy for us, and we won the Cup, and it seemed like the fans wanted to run him out of town. I thought he did a remarkable job in the role he played for our team in that Cup run. I think it was one of the best trades Peter Chiarelli made that no one ever talks about.

If You Were Commissioner, Would You Eliminate Fighting from the NHL? No. Absolutely not.

A game without fighting becomes a pressure cooker. You're on a 200-by-85-foot ice surface, emotions run high, people are moving fast, and sometimes a fight is the only thing that can keep the game from getting completely out of hand.

I was fortunate enough to have lunch with Dana White a few years ago. I flew out to Las Vegas to meet with him to see if we could get a UFC event in the Panthers' building. Either Matt Caldwell or I asked Dana how he even came up with the UFC idea, and he said, "If a fight broke out in this restaurant right now, what do you think everyone would do? Simple. Everyone would stop, watch the commotion, and see what happens. They would watch the fight. It's *human instinct!*"

Whether you agree with the premise or not, it's the same thing in a hockey game. It *is* entertaining. I've never seen anyone sitting down during a hockey fight.

What Sport Would You Play If Not Hockey? I've become friends with a lot of golfers, so I wish I was good enough to take my game to *that* level.

But growing up, my second sport was lacrosse and I really loved that game. My cousins, Zach and Ryan, played professionally, and it's just not a way to make a full living. But I love the sport.

The Highlight of My Career: Without a doubt, the two Stanley Cups, but for different reasons. One was more exciting and one just means more.

The Bruins Stanley Cup win means more to me because I was part of the rebuilding process and I was part of the leadership team. I like to think I played a hand in resetting the culture within that dressing room. Of course, I was also fortunate enough to play some meaningful minutes that year, even in Game 7 of the Final.

Anaheim was more exciting because 12 months earlier I had been debating retirement. A year later, I'm in Anaheim, my first full year in the NHL, and we're winning the Stanley Cup. And the retirement talk was legit. I had already begun skating with cops in Toronto and Erin had already passed her police testing. Erin and I decided I would give it one more year, and I signed a one-year deal with Anaheim. If I didn't make the NHL coming out of that contract, we were going to move back to Oshawa and become police officers.

The Best Teammate I Ever Had: That is such a tough question because I've had so many great teammates. I guess the guys I'm still best friends with and still have a strong relationship with to this day would be at the top of the list. Guys like Tuukka Rask, Shane Hnidy, P.J. Axelsson, Patrice Bergeron, and Terran Sandwith. But that's just off the top of my head, and there are many, many others.

Any Regrets from Your Career? We've already talked about the Brooks Orpik incident, so we don't need to rehash that here.

But honestly, when I look at my career from a big-picture perspective, I don't think I have any regrets. I certainly could have worked a lot harder as a younger player before I straightened my life out. Everything happens for a reason. I got to play until I was 40 years old. I don't think if I had been in the NHL when I was 22 I would have played until I was 40.

Am I hard on myself? Do I wish I could have scored more? Sure. But I have no complaints and no regrets. On the whole, I was blessed.

Advice for Being a Good Teammate: I remember I spent two Christmases by myself in Anaheim and in Chicago. I'm Canadian, so American Thanksgiving didn't mean as much to me, but I spent several of those alone too. So when Erin and I got to Boston, we made it our mission to make sure that didn't happen to anyone else.

Anyone who didn't have anywhere to go for a holiday, either to see family or have family coming into town, came to our house so they could be around people who cared about them. We didn't have kids back then, so that included Christmas Eve. We could have a real *shaker* for Christmas Eve because we didn't have to worry about waking up the kids. Fortunately I had a wife who felt the same way.

I'm not sure if we understood if it meant much to all the guys, but a guy like Looch made it clear it did. He sends me a picture every Thanksgiving saying, "Happy Thanksgiving to you and E-Train!" But we always did it because we thought it was the right thing to do, not because we were looking to have a profound impact on guys' lives. I've been lonely around the holidays and I just never wanted anyone else to feel like that.

The Most Physically Intimidating Player I Ever Saw: I would have to say Zdeno Chara, Derek Boogaard, or John Scott, just because of their size and mass.

I know Andy Ference once said Z could probably kill someone if he wasn't careful, and I think that's true. I don't know what kind of shape Boogaard and Scott were in, but I played with Z for seven years and I know what that man did day to day. Maybe because I know him so well, and like him so much, he isn't as intimidating to me. Plus, before

I played with Z, I never played against him, other than in the minors a couple of times. But if I'm on the other side, I'm gonna think he's as scary as anyone in the game.

The One Person I Got to Meet Who Impressed Me: I'm very lucky. I've been able to meet some very cool people because of what I do for a living. I can never limit this to just one person.

The fact that Bobby Orr calls me and we're actually friends still blows me away. In my opinion he's the greatest to ever play and the greatest human being that I've ever met. I'll admit that Bobby is my *holy s—t* moment.

Padraig Harrington is on my list. My wife and I went to Dublin and went out to dinner with him and his wife. Growing up as a golf fan and being of Irish descent, having dinner with Padraig was a very cool moment for me.

I know Keegan Bradley very well. He was the defending champion at the PGA Grand Slam of Golf in 2012 in Bermuda. He invited Erin and me to fly over and watch him compete. Keegan basically made us part of his family for the weekend. We stayed with them at the Fairmount and walked around the course with his wife, Jill.

When the tournament was over, we stayed at the hotel for one last night and ended up going to the restaurant and bar. Padraig was an alternate getting into the tournament that year and actually ended up winning. I had played with Padraig just the month before at the Deutsche Bank Open at TPC in Norton, Massachusetts. We ended up running into each other and joining up with them that night. So Erin and I were celebrating Padraig's tournament win with him; his wife, Caroline; and his caddie, Ronan Flood.

Everyone knows I'm a huge boxing fan—not hard to figure out given what I did for a living. After we won the Cup in 2011 my friend Tom Buckley introduced me to legendary boxing trainer Freddie Roach. Freddie ended up asking us to come out to Las Vegas to see the Manny Pacquiao–Timothy Bradley fight.

I was in Vegas with my boxing coach Tommy McInerney and Eric Tosi, who worked for the Bruins at the time. We got invited to a dinner at The Four Seasons, and in the room with us were Freddie, Jim Lampley, Jalen Rose, Max Kellerman, and Freddie's security guy, who was a friend of Tommy's from Dedham. I was sitting in the room, looking around, and just thinking, *How the* hell *did I end up in a place like this, with these people?*

TOMMY McINERNEY
Shawn's boxing coach and friend

Freddie is a Boston guy. When we went out there, he acted like he had known Shawn for a long time. And Shawn didn't act like Freddie was someone different. We were all just ourselves, and I think Freddie respected that. Shawn talked to him like he was one of his teammates in the locker room. Shawn loved listening to the stories he was telling us. I also think Shawn and Freddie had similar upbringings. They both had to fight and claw their way to get to where they were. To this day, Freddie and Shawn are like best friends.

Since that time, I became friends with Freddie and he has supported the Thornton Foundation. Freddie even invited Tommy and me to come out to Los Angeles for a few days to train with him. We went to Freddie's gym, and he *really* put me through my paces. He has invited me to several of his big fights, and it's all because of playing for the Bruins in Boston, and I guess being a good person. Those are the moments the game of hockey has given me.

Erin and I were at a charity event in Boston, and she said to me, "Isn't that Kenny Florian over there?" We were both big fans of UFC and The Ultimate Fighter, so we went over to introduce ourselves and shake his hand. He couldn't have been nicer, and we ended up becoming really good friends. In fact, I started jujutsu training because of Kenny.

One night, we were sitting at Ironsides having a beer, and I simply asked him, "Hey, what happens if we take this outside?" Kenny, the nicest and most humble individual in the world, said, and I'm paraphrasing, "Thirty seconds, Thorty. Listen, we square off and you hit me on the way in, I'm in one and maybe I could be in trouble. I'm well aware of how tough you are. But what you don't know is I'm probably going to start by kicking you in the leg, and you're not trained for that. I'm going to take you to the ground because I'm a fifth-degree black belt, then I'm going to put you to sleep in about 30 seconds."

Now that I've studied jujutsu for the past nine years, I realize that Kenny was exaggerating. He said it would take him 30 seconds to take me out, but he could probably do it in 20.

When we were playing the Canucks in the Stanley Cup Final, there was a UFC fight in Vancouver as well, and Kenny was on the card fighting for the belt with Diego Nunes. Shane Hnidy and I went over to his hotel to visit with him and he asked for a favor. He wanted to wear my Bruins jersey to the weigh-in.

I believe the weigh-in was the same day as Game 2, and he went out on the stage wearing a Shawn Thornton jersey. The Bruins-Canucks series was already pretty heated at that point, so Kenny got booed off the stage! I still have the picture of Kenny on the scale wearing a Bruins jersey with my number on the back. *That* was a very cool moment. I certainly never expected to have that happen in my life.

Being on set with Seth MacFarlane—I'm a huge *Family Guy* fan—was unbelievable. Having a glass of wine in Mark Wahlberg's trailer while we were waiting to film was unreal. Those are the moments that I'm not in awe of, but I also don't ever take for granted. I always think that my friends from Oshawa would be saying, "Holy s—t!" if they were there with me.

CHAPTER 17

THE ELEPHANT IN THE ROOM

IT'S PROBABLY TIME to address the elephant in the room, and that's the toll taken when you do what I did for a living.

I'm the exact opposite of some guys you've heard about in the NHL. I'm not going to blame anything that happened to me, or the effect it might have on me, on the sport of hockey and the way I played it. I knew full well the job I signed up to do. It sucked sometimes, but I was happy to do it. I'm not giving the houses and the money back. I did what I had to do.

I know a guy like P.J. Stock—who I have a lot of respect for—has wondered if he's just getting older or if he's taken too many shots to the head. That's the difference between us. I didn't put myself in a position to take too many shots to the head.

TOMMY McINERNEY
Shawn's boxing coach and friend

I actually think Shawn could have done real well if he was in my world. He has that fighter mentality, and his work ethic is just unbelievable. He's very smart, but he's also smart with his hands. Boxing is the sweet science, and you don't waste punches. The really good boxers pick their shots, and they throw punches with a purpose. When I first started sparring with Shawn, I could see that every time he threw a punch it was about as accurate as it could be. He showed me things early on that you would normally only see in a veteran fighter.

There weren't very many times when I worried about the toll the game, and my style of play, was taking on my body. I mean, my hands, probably yes. Shoulders, yes. My neck, maybe a little bit. I can also tell you with 100 percent certainty that I was never worried about my head.

I remember talking to Milan Lucic when he was just a kid coming up, and I told him it's not how many fights you win that matters, it's how many you *don't* lose. I really, truly believe that. I was a defense-first type of guy. When I was younger I might have been a little bit different, but as I matured I learned that you've got to learn to pick your spots. You'll win more than you lose, but try and be smart about not getting hit.

MILAN LUCIC
Bruins teammate

I was a physical power forward who could also drop the gloves. But I was also 19 years old coming from juniors and fighting guys pretty much my own age, and now I was facing men. Thorty helped me out so much just in that way. He took care of certain guys and I took care of other guys. I think we were a pretty big part of bringing back that identity.

I would always watch Shawn to see what techniques and methods he would use. He was usually fighting guys who were taller and bigger than him, but he never got the credit he deserved for how good of a technical fighter he was and how smart he was. He never put himself in a position to really get tagged with a huge punch. The way he protected himself, and the way he would hold onto guys when he needed to. Shawn was a natural lefty, but he could switch up on you and throw with his right hand as well. I used to just watch him, and I got to learn so much from that.

In my mind, I had really good defense and I didn't get hit too often, unless I was fighting way out of my weight and length range. Thankfully, those moments were few and far between.

I think I was actually concussed twice, or maybe three times. John Scott was one. But I recovered from that one *so* fast that it didn't seem like it could be a real concussion. I got hit behind the ear, and it felt more like vertigo than a concussion. That's the one after which I asked MMA fighter Kenny Florian for his advice. I felt off that evening, and I had some memory lapses, but the next day I felt pretty good and two days later I felt perfectly fine. Maybe it was a concussion and maybe it wasn't. It was deemed a concussion.

ERIN THORNTON
Shawn's wife

Early in his career, Shawn got called up for a little bit after the start of the season, and that was the first time I ever got a real taste of how Shawn made his living. He ended up fighting this massive human being—I think it might have been Georges Laraque—and I say to this day that he threw Shawn *over* the boards and into his own bench. Shawn will deny that vehemently, by the way.

I was sitting next to Nathan Dempsey's wife. She could tell I was a little concerned about what was happening. She grabbed my leg and said, "Just so you know—if he goes to the penalty box and he sits down, he's fine. If he goes back to the bench, then down the hallway, if it's *really* bad, someone will call you." That was my first taste of real fighting in hockey.

I also remember talking when we got home that night. I said, "Thanks for telling me that's what you did for a living." He just said, "That's why you were sitting next to Nathan Dempsey's wife." Then he said, "I'm fine, I'm fine." He just blew it off, like, *This is life. Get used to it.*

But the concussion I had in juniors when I was 18 years old, from Lee Cole, was by far the worst I ever had. I knew I was a mess, and I ended up having to get surgery on my busted nose. My parents drove me back to my billet after the game, and they had to pull over twice so I could puke.

I couldn't get out of bed for a month. I couldn't look at bright lights. I couldn't ride the bus with the team. It was completely different from anything I'd ever experienced before or since. Thank God, I never had that feeling again as a player.

I also understand if someone questions if I ever wondered what I might have been doing to the other guy. Honestly, I have to say yes and no. Going in, it's a job we both signed up for.

I remember a fight in the minors with a guy named Grant McNeill. I had a fairly big reputation by that time, and he was playing pretty hard on me. He gave me a cross-check I didn't like and I generally didn't fight mad too often, but that time I was upset. I hit him with a punch, and guys who hit people will understand, but it didn't even feel like I hit him.

He was *out cold.* He hit the ice like a stone. When he tried to get off the ice, he went to a place in the rink that didn't have a door. I felt bad. I felt really bad in that moment. When I went into a fight, I was never hoping to put someone in the hospital. I always went into it like a job, like a boxing match. Things can happen sometimes, and obviously I wanted to win the fight, but I also wanted to come out of it where no one was seriously hurt.

Hockey fighting to me is like a martial art. I respected the guys I went up against, and I tried to respect the code: don't do to him what you wouldn't want him to do to you. I wouldn't want someone to hit me while I was down. I would lose my mind, and I would seek vengeance for the rest of my life. I always tried to keep that in the back of my mind when I was fighting somebody else. If someone had a jersey over their head and couldn't see, I didn't feel it was a fair fight and I would let up.

Look, if we're standing toe-to-toe, man-to-man, throwing punches, I'm okay with that. We both knew what we signed up for. But when you put someone at a disadvantage that is out of their control—their tie-down snaps or their jersey is over their head—that's not something you can foresee or agree to. I wasn't a believer in taking advantage of that situation to hurt somebody. You take advantage of it by ending the fight—throwing him down, or putting him in a position where the linesman had to step in.

There were a couple of times when I asked the linesman to step in because I thought the other guy was in trouble. Krys Barch was one of those times. I saw his face did not look good and called the linesman in. One time a jersey came over Colton Orr's face, and I don't think he wanted to quit. He couldn't see and I could have kept throwing, and honestly I think Orrsy would have been fine with that, but he's wired a little different than me. I called the refs in, but I don't think Orr wanted to stop. But I'm also thinking, if I'm fighting Colton Orr again and my shirt gets up over my head and I can't see where the punches are coming from, I would hope he would have the respect to not break my face.

My internal wiring came first from my family, but was also cemented playing Sidewalk Square while training with Lionel. He taught me it was a job, but you're not trying to kill the other guy. Hey, even that game, as barbaric as it might sound, had rules. The biggest rule was, you were going to have to get back into that sidewalk square someday and maybe with the same guy. If you take advantage of someone it's going to come around. It *always* comes around. And the more you do it, the *quicker* it's going to come around if you're being an asshole.

I also don't believe too many guys took advantage of me. Jared Boll, who I've gotten to know since, landed an extra punch or two one time, and it threw me off. But s—t happens in a fight. I never remember being in a really precarious situation, where I couldn't defend myself, and someone taking advantage of that. Did guys throw an extra punch or two here or there? Yeah. Have I done it in the heat of the moment, or by accident? Probably. It was never my intention.

You've got to keep something in mind here too. Anxiety and fear are two different things. I was anxious a lot; there is *no* doubt about it. But I wouldn't say I was *afraid* of someone.

Take John Scott. If I was afraid of him, I probably wouldn't have fought him. But I was anxious for a long time going into that one. I'm not going to lie. I was anxious with Derek Boogaard. I was anxious any time I was fighting somebody for the first time. That was more the anxiety of not knowing exactly what you're getting into.

TERRAN SANDWITH
St. John's teammate

We were in training camp, and we were playing the Edmonton Oilers. I had been in that organization for three years before that. Shawn comes up to me before the game and he says, "Do you think I can beat Georges Laraque?" So I just told him, "Absolutely not. There is no way! He is going to destroy you. He is going to clean your clock."

So the first shift, Shawn goes right after him, and Georges cleans his clock and just throws him around. I talked to Shawn in the dressing room after the period and I said, "Shawn, what did I just tell you? You can't beat that guy!" Shawn looks at me and he says, "You know what? I think I can beat him!" He never stopped trying and I think every time they fought, Shawn lost *a little less* each time. Eventually he beat Georges because I think he just willed himself to beat Georges.

When I came into the game, there was no HockeyFights.com. You would go into a fight literally not knowing if the other guy was a lefty or a righty, if he threw heavy hands, if he could switch. You went into those fights thinking, *I'll have to figure this out as I go along*. A fear of the unknown creates the anxiety.

There were a lot of sleepless nights, and a lot of skipping game day naps, trying to cope with the anxiety. That *does* exist. I'm also not going to complain about it. People in all walks of life have anxiety.

Another cause of anxiety is having to play against guys you've been teammates with and worrying about what-ifs. Take Looch, for example. We're *very* close friends, and he certainly knows how I'm wired. When we're out there, if the situation arises, it's our job to put personal friendships aside and do what needs to be done. We can be friends again afterward. I know he's wired the same way. It never happened, and it never went to that place.

MILAN LUCIC
Bruins teammate

I played three years against Shawn after we both left the Bruins, and I'll be honest, I thought about what would happen if we had to square off. You're always ready, but thankfully it never got to that point. It's funny; being Thorty's teammate, I had seen him fight guys he had played with in the past. You kind of saw how he handled it—what happens on the ice stays on the ice. It's just guys doing their job. If it had ever come down to that, both of us would definitely have our guard up, and probably would *not* have enjoyed it. But we would have done it, if it came down to it.

I've fought friends of mine plenty of times. I didn't like it, and they probably didn't either. I certainly would not have wanted to fight Looch. He's a *tough* guy! It's not like I was the older vet and helped groom him, so I'm just going to go into a fight with him and pick him apart. He has heavy, quick hands. He's a beast of a human being. He walks around at 240 pounds on a comfortable day. He would have been no walk in the park, that's for sure!

Travis Moen was a real good friend of mine. We were roommates in the minors and also in Anaheim. I had to fight him when he was in Montreal, and I definitely picked the fight. Mo is a tough kid, and he was fine, but I truly don't think our friendship has been the same since. I probably ruined a friendship for the cause.

But I also don't regret it, not for one second. We may have fallen out anyways, just because he retired a couple of years later and went back to Saskatchewan. We just didn't see much of each other. Was it that, or was it because I instigated a fight with him? I don't think Mo is like that, and I think—actually, I *know*—if we got together tomorrow, we would be having beers and joking about it like nothing ever happened.

I felt bad at the time. I called and texted him to tell him that I felt terrible. And to his credit, he said, "Thorty, don't even worry about it. I get it. It's our job." But he also used to come to my house for dinner every single time he came to town, and that didn't happen anymore after the fight.

Other than the Brooks Orpik incident, I don't think I ever really instigated anything at the NHL level just for the hell of it. It was probably different back in my younger and wilder AHL days. When I was playing for St. John's, I was trying to follow in the footsteps of a guy like Greg Smyth. Sometimes you had to act like you had a screw loose to give yourself enough room to do what you had to do on a normal day.

I watch the game from a different perspective now, and I see that some people express concerns about head trauma, concussions, CTE—and the long-term effects on the players. But as I said earlier, we all sign up for this and we all get the benefits of being NHL players.

I understand the concern, but we all make choices in life, and playing in the NHL, the AHL, or professional hockey generally is a choice. It's a dream come true for a lot of young men all around the world.

Are there risks to playing the game? Of course there are. But there are risks everywhere. My friend Dave Duerden goes into some bad neighborhoods every single day for his job. He takes a calculated risk every single day when he shows up to work as a police officer. I have friends who are paramedics and firefighters. They have to jump into burning buildings! I have a hard time finding a way of life that doesn't involve some sort of risk.

At least if you're an athlete you get the best care, the best medical coverage. We have trainers with us every day to take care of us. We get paid an incredible amount of money to play games for a living.

The game definitely moves fast, and there are some big hits. Do I think there's still a place for fighting? *One hundred percent.* The game is a pressure cooker, and fighting helps remove the lid and relieve some of that pressure.

I also know there has been a lot of discussion of the instigator penalty in hockey. I honestly think the change was necessary at the time. Now I think we've gotten to a point where you could maybe go back to the rule the way it used to be. We might need to go back and curb some of the cheap shots and stuff.

TRENT YAWNEY
Head coach, Norfolk Admirals and Chicago Blackhawks

If someone on our team was getting picked on, Shawn would *always* be the first to respond. As much as our game has changed, that part has been lost a little bit. I don't think players pay as much attention to protecting teammates as they used to. But it's an important aspect of the game, and Shawn was very good at it. If one of our young guys was getting picked on, Shawn was always in there. He wasn't necessarily fighting, but he would stick his nose in there and basically say, "If this is going to continue, you're gonna have to answer to somebody and that somebody is going to be me." His favorite line was always, "Slow your roll!"

I also think the equipment factor is important in the game right now. I think some heads and shoulders are potentially at risk from factors beyond fighting and the instigator rules. I don't think too many guys are afraid of throwing their shoulder into someone at 25 miles per hour because they feel so protected. And with that you're going to have the ripple effect of whiplash, concussions, sternum injuries, etc.

I told ESPN one time that I felt the majority of concussions in the NHL came from guys moving 35 miles per hour and open-ice hits with huge shoulder pads on. I never wore those pads. I felt better without them. I felt I could skate better and I could fight better, when I had to. I *did* feel that if 90 percent of the league wore those smaller shoulder pads we would have a lot fewer concussions, and I stand by that.

Everyone makes their own decisions. A lot of guys wore the smaller pads in practice, and I think maybe Z wore the same pads as me.

Look, I didn't hit people too hard. I finished my checks, but I wasn't a guy who laid people out, so I wasn't too worried about *my* shoulders. Guys who lay people out are probably worried about their shoulders.

Overall, I think the game is in a pretty good space right now. If I was in charge, would I dial back some of the protective measures involving shoulders and elbows to keep people a little more in check? Yeah, probably. I understand the counterargument. Both guys should be equally protected, but it seems a little much at times.

I'm not a doctor. I'm just somebody who played the game for a long time and survived it. I understand that some guys haven't been as lucky in that regard. This is a tough one to articulate, but there are many factors involved for those guys who haven't been as lucky. Some guys didn't protect themselves as well. Some guys didn't hold other people accountable for their actions or give themselves an edge and give people pause before they ran through someone. To be completely honest, I survived as long as I did because people might have been a little bit afraid of me.

I was not the best puck handler, and I skated with my head down half the time. But you would be hard-pressed to find too many guys who were going to take a run at me for fear of what I might have done if they didn't get all of me!

AL MacADAM
Head coach, St. John's Maple Leafs

I fought in the NHL, but I fought to survive. I fought so I could play, but Shawn fought so other guys could play. I put a letter on his sweater because, even though he was very young and still immature in some ways, he had leadership qualities. He always played to win and he saw the big picture. You cheer for guys like Shawn. He might not have had high-end skill, but you saw something right away that might get him there.

Take a guy like Patrice Bergeron. I'm sure opposing players weren't as afraid of him as they might have been of me. Patrice did get hit from behind one time, very badly. I thought the hit from Randy Jones was a cheap shot. Unfortunately, those things are going to happen in our sport or any other. There is no such thing as utopia in our sport, and you can never get rid of all the badness.

But do I think Randy Jones would have taken a run at me if my numbers were facing him? Probably not. Is that right or wrong? No, it's just reality. He took advantage of Bergy in that situation, and it still pisses me off that I wasn't able to give a receipt for that. Things are going to happen.

PATRICE BERGERON
Bruins teammate

On the ice, Shawn was like a big brother for players like me, Marc Savard, David Krejci, and others. I can recall many times when a guy would lay a big hit on me or someone else, and when the guy came back to his bench, Shawn would be waiting for him at the door to our bench, letting him know that was the last time in that game he would be hitting one of us like that. He would simply say, "If you do that again, you're going to have to deal with me." As a player, Shawn let you feel more comfortable and more confident. We knew he had everybody's back, and that had a big impact on the other team.

It's a f—ing hard game to play! We'll never get to a position where everyone is safe. Even if you completely got rid of contact, things would still happen.

I have a wife and two daughters and nothing matters more to me than they do, but I honestly don't worry about my future with them and maintaining my faculties. Do my knees and hips hurt some days? Yeah, but that comes from just being a hockey player, not a fighter. My hands hurt most of the time, but it's manageable. My head is fine. Maybe I'm just being naive, but I don't worry about that part. I actually have a ridiculous memory, and I don't forget much. I pay attention, and I don't space out. Call me in 20 years, and maybe I'll tell you something different, but that's how I feel right now.

I'm happy that I was able to use my physicality to set myself up in a place where both of my daughters are going to have their college educations paid for before they even get there. They can grow up in a nice neighborhood. I'm around on weekends. I have a job that allows me to take them to gymnastics here and there. I'm happy to be in a position where I can take them to the arena, or where Stanley, the Florida Panthers team mascot, came over to the house for Halloween. I'm happy I've been able to put myself in a position where my family can reap some of the benefits of what I did to make a living and my hard work.

CHAPTER 18

THE NEXT STEP

I WASN'T SURE WHAT WAS GOING to happen with the Bruins after the 2013–14 season. There was a lot of uncertainty. We had just lost the playoff series to the Canadiens, and the game looked like it was starting to move in a different direction. Whether it was or not is probably a matter of perception.

I was actually on the golf course with Jarome Iginla and James Driscoll. We were playing Charles River and Peter Chiarelli shot me a text and just said, "Hey would you mind swinging by the office tomorrow." It was around June 14 or 15, and I assumed it wasn't good news. My agent hadn't been talking with Peter about renewing or extending my deal.

I went home and tried to put it in the back of my mind. There was no use sitting and worrying about something that was out of my hands and wouldn't happen until the next day. I figured I would just get my answer tomorrow. I never wanted to leave Boston, and neither did Erin, but if it happened I figured I could still at least get a job in the league.

The next day I got up and worked out like normal. I went to the Garden to see Peter. He basically thanked me for everything I had brought to the organization. He was very complimentary of all the things I had done in the community, off the ice, to help the franchise. He said he appreciated all the things I had done on the ice too, and he went out of his way to assure me that the decision had nothing to do with the suspension I had received earlier in the year. He said it was a tough decision, but they felt it was time to move on.

I really appreciated the conversation. I mean, I got to spend seven years in that city. For a guy with my role, I never knew how long I was going to be in any one place. Had I dreamed about playing another couple of years and retiring a Bruin, maybe taking a run at another Cup? Sure, I had. But it wasn't meant to be.

He asked me, "What can I do to help you out here?" I told him I didn't know what interest there was around the league in my services, but that I hoped if there was interest he would at least speak kindly of me. My memory was that he simply said tell me your top three choices of where you want to play next. I said Florida, Tampa, and Arizona. I had put up with seven New England winters, and I figured if I couldn't play for the Bruins, I at least wanted to enjoy some nice weather.

I really liked what Dale Tallon had been doing with the Florida organization. I paid attention, and I liked where the Panthers were going as well. I felt like they were on an upward swing, and I knew Dale from my time in Chicago.

Bruins vice president Matt Chmura told me that when I left Peter's office, he picked up the phone and called Dale. He told him, "Thorty is leaving us, and his first pick for a place to play is with you." Dale simply told Peter that they wanted me, and that certainly helped. Peter did me a tremendous solid.

MATT CHMURA
Vice president, Boston Bruins

Everyone talks about that first free-agent class of Savvy and Z, and those guys helped rebuild the talent in the organization, but Shawn was one of the guys who helped rebuild the culture. We got Andy Ference that March, but he didn't have any choice because he was traded here. He played a huge part in rebuilding the culture too. But Shawn, coming off his Cup win with

Anaheim, *chose* Boston. I know that Peter always appreciated what Shawn had done for the organization and there was a very real mutual respect. It was a healthy and mutual parting of the ways, and I think Peter felt if there was something he could do to help Thorty he was going to do it. So Peter called Panthers GM Dale Tallon to tell Dale that Shawn was interested in playing for the Panthers, and how much Shawn had meant to the Bruins, both on the ice and in the dressing room.

I called my agent, Anton Thun, right away and told him that the Bruins weren't bringing me back and that they were going to announce it in the next day or two. That was another solid by the Bruins organization. They certainly didn't have to go out and tell the hockey world that I was going to be a free agent two weeks before free agency even started. In my opinion that was a very classy move by them. They could have kept that quiet. I mean, who the f—k am I to warrant a press release or a person-to-person interview with Peter?

When we were allowed to talk, Anton had a chance to have a nice discussion with Dale. There were also a couple of other teams that expressed interest, but Anton said he and Dale sat down and agreed on a number within about 25 or 30 minutes. Anton called, and I just said, "That works for me. Let's go." It was one of the easier contracts of my entire career.

Vinnie Viola and Doug Cifu had just bought the team, and they had been at the game when the Bruins played the Panthers. I scored this absolutely ridiculous goal, and I think I might have fought that game too. I guess they looked at each other and said, "Who is this guy?!" So I was on their radar.

I didn't make my decision just based on nice weather in South Florida. I had seen what Dale had been able to do in Chicago, and as I said, I was impressed with the direction he had the team going. When I played against Erik Gudbranson, Aleksander Barkov, Nick Bjugstad, Jonathan Huberdeau—I could see these guys were young, but you could just tell they were going to be good players. Dale had a lot of good draft picks that I thought he would be able to utilize, and I just felt we were going to be pretty good within a couple of years.

Fast-forward to my second year with the Panthers, and I think we were one or two points out of the President's Trophy. We were a really good team and Dale was committed to adding to a very impressive young nucleus. We had Willie Mitchell, Jussi Jokinen, Derek MacKenzie, and we were bringing in some strong leaders who play the game the right way. A couple of us had won and knew how to win. Dale had brought Roberto Luongo in from Vancouver, so we were strong in goal. I had a pretty good idea where the organization was heading, and I wanted to be a part of it.

Of course, Roberto and I had some history after that Stanley Cup Final series in 2011. I didn't really know him. I knew he was a funny guy from other people. The rivalry was with Vancouver, and knowing Lou now as I do, how he got quoted during that Final series was *completely* out of context. I know now he was completely rattled about it.

There was no animosity whatsoever when we finally met. From day one I loved the guy. He chirps me all the time. When the Bruins did that Zoom reunion for the anniversary of the Stanley Cup win, Lou tweeted, "This is what my nightmares look like!" He is a funny, funny, funny guy. His Twitter feed is hilarious, and I can tell you that's him, not someone doing it for him.

I had become really good friends with PGA pro Keegan Bradley over the years, and he's on the board for my foundation. He and Brendan Steele were playing together on the tour in Los Angeles when they saw that I was might sign with the Panthers. Brendan knew Dale, and I knew Keegan, so they got him on the phone and Keegan told Dale that if he signed me, he would buy season tickets. I think he might still owe us some season tickets!

I was on my way to play at the Essex County Club when Keegan and Brendan called me on the speaker phone and said, "We just called Dale

Tallon and told him he had to sign you. We even told him we would buy season tickets!" I guess I had a couple of people going to bat for me.

When it happened, Dale was joking around with me. He said, "I told you I would get you back. I gave you your first f—ing contract!" He did try to sign me when I signed with the Bruins, and I was told he had inquired about me a couple of times while I was playing in Boston. He knew I had been a leader in the minor leagues, but the NHL is a different level. He said that I had developed as a player and as a leader. He said, "Just bring you. I want to teach these f—s how to win!"

When I told Erin we were signing with the Panthers, she was in tears, and in a bad way. She had friends in Boston, and we had been there for seven years. With a few call-ups back and forth, I had five years in Norfolk. I had one year in Anaheim, and we were apart most of the year. But then we had seven years in Boston, and it became home. It wasn't easy to leave.

If you ask her now, she'll tell you she loves living here in South Florida, but at the time it was hard. Erin is a homebody, through and through, and she loves where she is and embraces it.

We didn't have any kids at the time, but we did have a couple of dogs, and now we were uprooting and moving to a new state, a new city, and a new team. She was leaving friends and neighbors in Charlestown, and they weren't moving to Florida with us. But we found a house on a golf course and fixed it up. It took about six months to get it the way we wanted, so we lived in a vacation village for a while. Let's just say it was a tough start to our new life in Florida, but it all ended well.

It was certainly different than it had been in Boston. First, there weren't as many fans in the stands as you would like. It's common knowledge, but it also gets blown out of proportion a little bit. Our building is like the third biggest in the league, with more than 20,000 seats. Look, there were some tough nights at the start, like when we would be playing Ottawa on a Tuesday and have 5,000 people in the building. That was a little tough.

Ownership, rightly so, decided to strip all complimentary tickets in the market because it was totally out of hand, and we completely devalued our own product. Then as we got going as a team and started winning in my second year, the building was full again quite often. We definitely had a lot of games with 17,000 in there, which would be a sellout in a lot of other buildings.

We're players, and we feed off the energy brought by the fans in the building, but both teams have the same disadvantage, so it's just how you deal with it. You're expected to do your job, whether there is one fan in the stands, or 5,000, or 20,000. Those expectations were put to the test in the resumption of the 2020 season with *no* fans in the stands.

People forget that when I first got to Boston, we had around 11,000 people for our opener. People just think we had 20,000 people every night in an 18,000-seat arena, but it wasn't like that. We had games in Florida that had just as many fans as my first few games in Boston. Fans have a tendency to just forget those days now.

I knew that was going to be my last playing contract, but I had always given a lot of thought to what the next step was going to be. That's why I tried to learn as much of the business side as I could, even as a player. It's why I did a ton of speaking engagements and TV and radio appearances. I tried to build a brand for myself. I created my foundation. I was always thinking of what was to come.

My original thought was that I would get into the TV or radio end of the business. I had a lot of talks about that here in Florida, and I was actually in negotiations with NESN back in Boston. NESN offered me a three-year contract for when I retired. We were going to create a pregame show, something like me against the armchair quarterback. The idea actually came from something I had put on my audition reel. I had been on TV with Michael Felger after a Canucks game. A Vancouver reporter called in and I kind of went toe-to-toe with him. Most people felt that I had won the argument. The NESN people saw that and felt like it could be a fairly regular thing. Someone might call in and say,

"They've got to shoot more on the power play!" And I would break down the game in an easy-to-understand way. They thought that would be somewhat entertaining.

NESN also planned to use me as part of its pre- and postgame coverage. I had relationships with all of the other Boston organizations—the Patriots, Red Sox, and Celtics—and could perhaps cross-promote things with athletes from the other teams. I honestly thought that would be my next step. I got the offer around December of my second year in Florida, when I thought it was going be the last year I would play. That was my plan at the time.

At about that same time I sat down with Panthers president and CEO Matt Caldwell and minority owner Doug Cifu. When I first got here, the new ownership had just taken over. Matt was the COO at the time, and we hit it off right away. So the three of us sat down in a back office, and they told me they thought I was smarter than I let on. They thought I could be a valuable addition to the business side of the operation, but they weren't exactly sure yet what the role would look like. They thought I could help figure that out and just wanted to know if I was open to it. Doug told me to look at it as a "President in Training."

MATT CALDWELL
President and CEO, Florida Panthers
When Vinny Viola first bought the team, Shawn was one of the first players we brought in as a group of veterans to set the tone for our organization, and I saw what he did for our locker room as a player. We had some of our best years on the ice when Shawn was on our team, and we came to see what a valuable asset he was to our organization. We also grew to love him personally, so when he was coming to the end of his career, we attempted to figure out a path for him to stay with us. Shawn had shown an interest in the business side of our operation, which is a little uncommon for former players, who often go into hockey operations.

> Shawn has an innate intellectual curiosity and a great business mind, and we thought that with those qualities he would be an asset for our organization, but to be honest, he's been even better than we ever expected.

It was a good problem to have. I had two job offers at the same time I was working on my regular career. I started thinking that my passion was the business side of sports, and what I always wanted to get into, but I didn't think anyone would give me the opportunity. On the other hand, I had the chance to go back to Boston, and I still missed it there. It wasn't an easy decision.

My wife was a huge part of this decision as we were going through all the pluses and minuses. There were a lot of sleepless nights, but good sleepless nights. There are *way* worse problems in this world than the one I had. She said she just didn't see me going into television, sitting behind a desk and chirping fans for a living and explaining the game. That would involve almost being neutral and she said she knew me well enough to know I needed a vested interest in order to be passionate about it.

She told me I wasn't wired that way, and I just thought, *F—k, she's right!* I'm *not* wired that way. I'm not great at critiquing people, and by that I mean calling people out for their mistakes. It's just not how I'm built. Joseph Maar of NESN saw me in that role and sent me a contract that I never ended up signing. I think I would have eventually figured it out, but I probably prefer radio to TV. I'm not comfortable being in front of the camera, and I certainly don't like being the center of attention. I might have been decent at it, but it was never my passion.

I learned my lessons. My first couple of weeks in the office, when I didn't know who anyone was, I was *very* uncomfortable. I walked in, sat at my desk in the middle of the sales floor, and thought to myself, *What the f—k am I doing here?!*

I spent the next seven months doing just that and not knowing fully what my role was. I just invited myself to *every single meeting.*

"Hey, I'm Shawn. What do you do here?"

"I'm the VP of Sales."

"Perfect. When's your meeting? Can you add me to that? Thank you."

"Hey, I'm Shawn. What do you do?"

"Corporate sponsorships and partnerships."

"I've always been interested in corporate sponsorships. I would love to be in your meetings."

"Love to have you! Come with me. You can be in every meeting!"

It was like that all the time, with almost every department. Sales, sponsorships, marketing, public relations. That's all I did for three or four months.

I reported to Matt, who was doing kind of what I'm doing now, and he invited me to meetings and I would sit in, but I didn't really have a daily routine. And Matt was busy *working* every day! He didn't have to take the time and trouble to babysit me.

Charlie Torono, who helped out with partnerships and has a lot of knowledge and experience in the sports world, gave me some tasks to work on, and that really helped. I worked out a deal with Fanatics to get a store in the arena. I worked on an ownership advisory group, which never really came to fruition, with some of our biggest partners.

We were going into the celebration of our 25ᵗʰ anniversary, and I asked Matt if I could run point on everything we were going to do for the anniversary. I had enough contacts around the league, and I could call around. I could use some best practices, I could use the teams that I was working with—public relations, marketing, game presentation—and I could set up a committee.

The first big thing I did on the corporate side was to retire Wayne Huizenga's name in the rafters at the Arena. We had put Bill Torrey's name up there, which was well deserved, but Mr. Huizenga hadn't been recognized by the organization. He hadn't been to the arena in a long, long time, but he had brought the franchise there and he did *so* much for the community. I also felt there was a lot of similarities between Wayne Huizenga and the Viola family—how community-minded they are and how much they give back.

We would use this as a precursor to the 25th anniversary celebration. I ran point for Wayne Huizenga night, and it ended up being one of our most successful nights of the year. My efforts were noticed by some people who thought, "You know what? Maybe he *is* smarter than we think."

My position within the organization just sort of progressed from there. The team and I had set up what the 25th anniversary celebration was going to look like. We created Legacy Saturdays and brought back alumni every week to drop the first puck and celebrate their contributions to the organization. I was involved in the development of the anniversary logo and Vinny's son, John Viola—a *very* creative guy—got involved at the end and helped shape it into its final form.

Then we had that awful, terrible tragedy at Marjory Stoneman Douglas High School, and I was asked to handle everything involving the organization for that. I had been in Boston at the time of the Boston Marathon bombings and had seen how important the professional sports organizations were in the healing process. I *really* leaned heavily on the network of people who had done so much following that tragedy.

Later, the executive team plus me travelled to New York for meetings. Matt and others pointed out that all of the different departments—public relations, foundation, community relations, game presentation, marketing—had to work well, together, for the various causes and projects that I had been in charge of, and they *did.* They said these departments executed well and worked together better with me than they had in the past. So they put me in charge of those departments from then on.

And, don't take that "in charge" thing the wrong way. I have some remarkably smart people working with me who do most of it, and I just try to make sure everyone is communicating and working well together. I have to make the final decisions, the hard ones, that not everyone likes. It's great when everyone loves them but it doesn't always work out that way. But I'm in charge of managing the departments.

I only know this management team here in Florida, but I can tell you there are a lot of similarities between the culture of a hockey team and the culture of *this* management team. There is a lot of managing personalities, and I went through 22 years of that being a leader in the locker room. I think that experience pays a lot of dividends for me, personally, in my current position.

As a player, you know some guys need to be patted on the back, and others respond better to a kick in the ass. You know some people prefer that you be upfront and strict, or even blunt. Some players like to be challenged, others hate being challenged. It is important to recognize that how you approach each person individually affects the greater good of the whole, or in this case the organization. I think there are a *lot* of similarities in managing people on both sides of my hockey experience.

CHAPTER 19

GIVING BACK

MY INTRODUCTION TO HOSPITAL visits and giving back to the community really began with the St. John's Maple Leafs. The organization was very big on community involvement. A bunch of guys and myself went on a hospital visit. I remember going room to room and the kids were so excited to see all of us from the hockey team.

I walked into a room and my heart just stopped. Sitting in a chair on a respirator was Robyn, the 15-year-old daughter of Dick Hancock, who was the owner of Green Sleeves. I had become very close with both Dick and Carla Hancock. Their son, Stefan, owned Turkey Joe's, another place that I loved to frequent, and I also got to know Robyn's sister, Erin. I had been to dinner at their house just a week earlier and I had no idea that Robyn was sick at all. Robyn had cystic fibrosis and I didn't know. It was my first hospital visit, and this one hit close to home.

I spoke to Dick and Carla about seeing her there, but they just said, "Thorty, she's there all the time!" When I saw her at her brother's house for dinner she seemed perfectly normal to me and now I was visiting her as a patient in a children's hospital.

My experience with Robyn was probably the reason why I took to making hospital visits and why they were so important to me for the rest of my career. Robyn actually passed away while I was still playing in St. John's, and at Green Sleeves they named the second floor The Robyn's Nest.

Before writing this book, I'm not sure I ever pulled the threads together about why hospital visits meant so much to me. I know I love doing them, and I know how much I want to help those kids, but it all seems to go back to that visit in St. John's and seeing Robyn in that room.

When I first got to Boston, I really wanted to be a helpful voice for children in need. Before I got to know the lay of the land, I used to bounce around a lot and go from place to place. If you're not from Boston, you probably don't know the difference between Children's Hospital, or Tufts Medical Center, or the Jimmy Fund. If you're not from there you have to learn, and I had to learn. As far as I was concerned, all I cared about was visiting kids and doing whatever I could to cheer them up.

MATT CHMURA
Vice president, Boston Bruins

The guys who get drafted here and come up through the system may understand a little more the importance of community involvement to our organization. But Shawn's philanthropy was rooted in him, and I certainly don't want the organization to take any of the credit for that. Shawn completely bought into being a Bruin.

As I learned more and more, I concentrated my time and efforts between the Jimmy Fund and Children's Hospital. But even then, I always worried about whether or not I was doing enough. I was there, but I was concerned about if I was there *enough*. I always felt like it wasn't enough. If I couldn't be there visiting kids every week, I felt bad about it. I really wanted to give back, and help people, but I never felt like it was enough.

LISA SHERBER
Director of patient and family programs, Jimmy Fund Clinic
I remember the first time I was told Shawn Thornton was coming in, and I'm thinking, *Great! Just what I need. This big, tough, mean guy coming to see my kids.* Then he came into the clinic and all I could think was, 'Are you kidding me? This guy is a marshmallow!' You saw immediately how big his heart was, and I never looked at him the same again. He would just pop in. He would call me, and say, "Hey, I'm in the area. Is it okay if I come in to see the kids?"

The fact that he was thinking of our kids and knowing that his visit could change someone's day tells you all about him.

When I had my day with the Stanley Cup, I carved out about three hours to spend at Children's Hospital. There's a picture on the foundation's website that was taken that afternoon.

KATIE DEVINE
Boston Children's Hospital
It is no small feat bringing the Stanley Cup into Children's Hospital, but Shawn called me when he had his day with the Cup, and said, "Katie, I want to bring it into the hospital." But it also speaks to who Shawn is. Here is *his* day with the Stanley Cup, and he wants to share it with the kids at Boston Children's Hospital. For all of us at the hospital it was just incredible to share the Cup, and Shawn, with everyone.

Believe it or not, there was actually a positive that came from the NHL lockout. I had been doing my charity golf tournament for a couple of years by that time. The Bruins had always helped me run my tournament, and I would make a donation to the Bruins Foundation too. Bob Sweeney, the executive director of the Bruins Foundation, and Erin McAvoy, who was there at the time, were huge in assisting me to get my tournament off the ground. I didn't know the first thing about it, and they were so giving.

Then the lockout happened in 2012, and I wasn't allowed to talk to anyone associated with the Bruins. At that time, I didn't know how long the lockout was going to last, and I didn't want to lose my golf tournament and all the good we were able to do for charities. So I was kind of forced, in a way, into making a decision, and we made the choice to start my own foundation.

When I established the Shawn Thornton Foundation, I really wanted to help people. I did it for all the right reasons, but the only reason I'm even talking about it here is to thank the people who worked so hard to get so much good done. The people on my board of directors are Tom Tinlin, Chuck Murphy, Christine McMahon, Michael Fallon, Sarah McKenna, Sarah Tracey, Daniel Waltz, Keegan Bradley, and Tuukka Rask. They all do this for all the right reasons, and I could never thank them enough. These people volunteer all of their time and no one takes a nickel from any of this. Every dime that comes in goes right back out, and that's the way it will always be. Those people should be the people getting the recognition because they do a ton of work.

The foundation was originally formed to raise money to fight diseases near and dear to my heart—specifically Parkinson's Disease and childhood cancer. The pediatric cancer component came about because I had enjoyed visiting kids so much and trying to put a smile on their faces at a horrendous time for them. I could never get those kids out of my head.

TOM TINLIN
Board of directors, Shawn Thornton Foundation

The American Parkinson's Disease Association named an award after Shawn. Now their "Volunteers of the Year" receive the Shawn Thornton Award. When they announced that at one of our golf tournaments, for the first time ever, he was speechless! He's doing all of this for the right reasons and is never asking for anything himself. He's even reluctant to ask anyone for help with anything.

The Parkinson's component was completely because of my grandmother. She battled Parkinson's for the last 14 years of her life, and she passed away while I was playing for the Bruins. We played a home game, and I jumped on a plane to get home for her services, then rejoined the team in Chicago after that. My grandmother was a huge part of my world, and seeing her go through all she had to go through for 14 years was anguishing for everyone in my family.

She went from the woman who used to sneak me a sip of whiskey on St. Paddy's Day and being the life of the party to shaking in a wheelchair. She would be in her home, and her arm would shake so uncontrollably that she couldn't control it, and it would bang into the side of her wheelchair. She couldn't control herself, and she couldn't even call out for help because the disease had taken her voice too. It affected me and made me want to help, and it still does.

Even now, my foundation probably has a bigger footprint in Boston than it does down here in Florida. It's not for lack of desire on my part to make it a bigger thing here in Florida, but I'm still much better known as a member of the Bruins than for the three seasons I spent playing for the Panthers.

We, as an organization, are still doing everything we can to break into the consciousness of the South Florida market. We're always competing for attention with the Dolphins, the Heat, and the Marlins. But we have to fight for that attention every day. When I was finishing my career here with the Panthers, I still visited the kids in the hospitals, but I simply didn't have the platform or the reach that I had in Boston. I spent seven years in Boston and developed the relationships with the medical community and the people and organizations that partnered with my golf tournament.

We've racked our brains, as a foundation, to figure out ways to raise money and help with deserving causes here in South Florida. We want to make an impact here, on the daily lives of people in South Florida, and we will.

Anyone who knows me, or who has *ever* known me, knows that I care about doing things the right way. I know Erin said nothing is going to get done involving me if you worry about who gets the credit and, as always, she is right. I don't do things for the publicity or for the credit; I do it because it's the right thing to do.

KATIE DEVINE
Boston Children's Hospital

One year we had a bunch of younger guys come in to visit the hospital for a group visit. Rookies sometimes don't know what they don't know, and several of them were considerably late getting there. After everyone finally arrived, one of the younger players looked at another player and said, "Are you telling Thorty, or am I?" I asked what they had to tell Shawn, and the player said, "We have to tell him that some of the guys were late because he's going to be *really* mad. Those guys are in trouble!" It hit me that as important as it was for Shawn to make a contribution on the ice, it was equally as important that players give back off the ice. He was adamant with teammates that you are *not* late for community events; you go and you give it your all. This is really important too. Now, I'll be honest, sometimes I've had to say, "Shawn, you've got to watch your language around the kids!" But that's just because he becomes so comfortable and acts like he's one of them. And he is.

In the aftermath of the Marathon bombing, I went to Kerry Collins, the Bruins' senior director of community relations, and I told her I wanted to help, but I didn't want *anyone* to know what I was doing. I spent a couple of days visiting the survivors, and I certainly wasn't the only one. There was a famous Hollywood actor, who I can't name, who was doing the same thing. He might not be comfortable with me saying it, but Bobby Orr was doing the same thing too. We all just wanted to help in any way we could.

I promise you, no one would have known from me or anyone in the Bruins organization that I was visiting survivors at the hospital in the aftermath of the bombings. We came off a road trip and got home in the early morning hours, and I went into the office and just starting grabbing everything I could get my hands on. Then I headed out to the hospitals to do whatever I could to make people feel better.

One of the people I visited was Jeff Bauman. Jeff is a badass. He was at the finish line, cheering for his fiancée, Erin Hurley, as she was about a mile away from finishing the Marathon. When the bombs went off, Jeff was one of the more seriously injured people. Carlos Arredondo was also at the finish line, handing out American flags to the runners. He hopped the fence to offer aid, and he immediately went to help Jeff. Probably the most famous photo in the aftermath of the bombing was Carlos, helping Jeff, as he was being pushed in a wheelchair to the medical aid tent.

Jeff was in serious trouble when he arrived at the hospital, and doctors made the decision that both of his legs needed to be amputated immediately. He had lost so much fluid that doctors had to keep resuscitating him, keeping him alive until they could save his life in the operating room. He had both legs amputated in the early morning hours and was hanging on to life for a period of time.

After Jeff woke up he got word, through medical personnel, that he needed to talk to legal authorities. Despite being unable to speak, he was still able to give the FBI a description of Tamerlan Tsarnaev, who he had seen in the area of the attacks. Jeff's description helped the FBI utilize video surveillance footage and identify Tsarnaev as the likely Marathon bomber.

When I walked into Jeff's hospital room, there was another person there who I did not know. I was there to visit Jeff, offer my thanks, and any possible help I could as he moved forward to recovery. I didn't know the other person in the room was Gerry Callahan, morning co-host on WEEI Radio. He was also there to visit Jeff and offer his support.

The next day when Gerry went on the radio he told all of New England of my visit to Jeff. There was certainly no reason why he wouldn't—he didn't know I would have preferred to remain under the radar and behind the scenes. But now everyone knew I had been there, and that Jeff wasn't my only visit. I would *never* have told people I was there, but now everyone knew.

What we all went through in the aftermath of the Boston Marathon bombings shaped a lot of what I felt for a long time after that. In fact, it was those experiences that came to the forefront after the shootings at Marjory Stoneman Douglas High School when I was with the Florida Panthers. What I had really learned, more than anything else, was to just listen. The families here in Florida were going through the same things the families were going through in Boston. It was completely out of their control and they were trying to grapple with the question of, "Why did this happen to us?" Everyone had a different way of dealing with it, and I learned to just listen and honor what they had to say. I could never know what these families were going through, but I learned they were all going through it in their own way.

ERIN THORNTON
Shawn's wife

We had been living in Parkland, Florida, for just a short while when the school shooting took place. What happened at Marjory Stoneman Douglas was absolutely horrifying. The daughter of one of our neighbors was one of the children shot that day. You felt like you couldn't escape it. It was stressful for everyone, but Shawn was the point person for the Panthers after that and it was really stressful for him. He was so concerned about doing the right thing, not to do right by the Panthers, but to do right by the families.

There are a number of players from the Panthers who live in the community, and that includes my own family. The Alhadeff family lives three doors down and across the street from us. I see them every day, and their daughter, Alyssa, isn't there with them anymore. I still talk to Fred Guttenberg fairly regularly, and his daughter Jaime is no longer with us. Those girls were both 14 years old. If it was one of my daughters, I can't even imagine what it would be like.

After the shootings there were a number of phone calls, and our team president, Matthew Caldwell, asked me if I could run point on behalf of the Panthers. I was happy to do anything I could to help.

The first thing I did was reach out to Sarah McKenna of the Red Sox, and I can't put into words how she helped me get my arms around what had happened at Marjory Stoneman Douglas and helped shape how our organization was going to help the people in our community deal with it.

As soon as it happened, our team ownership told me, "Whatever you need, and whatever the community needs, you have it. We don't care what it costs. Anything the community needs, you make sure they have it."

MATT CALDWELL
President and CEO, Florida Panthers

After what happened at Marjory Stoneman Douglas, I told Shawn, "You have to go full-time on this and be our point person." He was tremendous.

He did so many things behind the scenes, talking to all those families. Shawn would never admit it and we would never publicize it, but I think all those families would attest to what Shawn did for all of them. Every single thing we tried, as an organization, to do to help came from Shawn Thornton. I know Shawn doesn't want to talk about it, and he's probably not happy with me that I am, but people need to know.

I spoke to a lot people who had been through a similar situation with Sandy Hook, and with people who had been through it with the Marathon bombings. It was clear immediately that money doesn't bring anyone's kids back. So the question for me became, what *can* I do? And the answer quickly revealed itself: just listen.

FRED GUTTENBERG
Shooting victim Jamie Guttenberg's father

Shawn has also spoken to me about being in Boston after the Marathon bombings. He was with the Bruins when that community needed consoling and needed someone who could try to understand what people were going through. I guess the right word is empathy and he had it Boston, and he had it in droves here. I'm not sure if it was because of what he experienced in Boston, but I actually think that's just who he is.

You let the community know that you are here for whatever they need—*whatever* it is—but don't pretend to think you know what that is. I won't get into everything we did on the record, but we were committed to doing *anything* we could do to help the people.

Not long after the tragedy, the Marjory Stoneman Douglas hockey team won the state championship here in Florida. Before the team went to the state championship, we arranged to bring the Stanley Cup out to their practice. The team had earned the right to go to nationals, so we went to team owner Vinny Viola and asked if we could help get the team to Minnesota. He didn't even hesitate. He just said, "Talk to the company we use to charter to the games," and he chartered a jet to get the team to Nationals.

Now, honestly, we wanted all of that stuff to remain closed-off and behind-the-scenes, but one of the local media outlets had gotten really involved with the team and a couple of the families, so they heard about it. Bonnie, who was the manager of the hockey team, is certainly not a PR person, and suddenly she's getting bombarded from everywhere—she's hearing from ESPN, HBO, *Sports Illustrated*, and a lot of other national media outlets as well. Everyone is calling her and asking her questions, and she was kind of overwhelmed.

So we tried to help her out too. We had already confirmed that the Stanley Cup was coming, so we offered to do just one media availability on that day, let everyone get their B roll and their behind-the-scenes stuff—the captains, a couple of kids on the team. Fred Guttenberg's son played on the team, and everyone was trying to get more reaction. We just said, "Let's just do one thing, and hopefully it will ease the stress on Bonnie and the kids." We were trying to take this on for them, and take the stress *off* of them, but we *hated* that we were out there in front of the school on this.

Later on, I believe it was the school's debate team that was supposed to go to Washington, DC, and we got word about it. Someone asked if we could help get teddy bears for the bus ride to Washington, just so the kids had something to hold onto. It's heartbreaking to even think about. So we went out and bought 150 Build-A-Bears, just to help the kids on their trip to Washington.

We helped arrange for a sit-down with some of the kids and Chris Martin, the lead singer of Coldplay. I was there, along with some of the police who were among the first responders to kick in the door at the school.

FRED GUTTENBERG
Shooting victim Jamie Guttenberg's father

Shawn also lives in Parkland. Every once in a while he would text me, just to check in. He texted me one time and just said, "Hey, why don't we meet for breakfast?" We were sitting in this coffee/breakfast place in Parkland about six months after all of this happened. We were having breakfast and just talking—a couple of friends—and Shawn was asking how all the families were doing. He asked me if I had thought about what the one-year mark was going to be like. He just quietly said, "Do you think maybe the Panthers should do something?" That led to a much larger conversation that led to the Panthers doing a one-year commemoration of the event.

We didn't do it on the 14th, because that was the night the families just wanted to be inside and private, but we did it on the 17th, when the Panthers played their next game. They had the 17 families to the game, and we all participated in the ceremonial puck drop. They honored the families with a *beautiful* video and the Panthers organization built a huge memorial inside the Den of Honor within their arena. Now every time people go to a game, they'll see this memorial. Shawn was the driving force behind all of this. This is his community. He knows me, he's gotten to know the other families, and while he may have been a tough guy on the ice, he's got the world's biggest heart off the ice.

We invited all of the families out to the first game after the tragedy happened, and to our surprise a lot of them actually showed up. Then came the opportunity, on the ice, for someone to speak on behalf of the Florida Panthers. Roberto Luongo was one of the guys, like me, who lived in Parkland, and it just seemed right that he speak on behalf of the organization. I reached out to Sarah McKenna and Charles Steinberg from the Red Sox for their help after what they had been through with the Marathon bombing. They made suggestions, and I cleaned it up some, but Roberto took it from there and just did an *amazing* job on the speech from the ice.

I think Lou knew that he had to do it, but he was very hesitant to take on something as important as that. His wife is from Parkland, and his kids grew up here, so he was the obvious choice.

On the one-year anniversary we created the first memorial to the kids, here in our arena. I had our creative director, Alex Lytle, sketching the faces of these children for five straight days.

We were putting 17 families, who had lost their children, in our arena on the one-year anniversary of it happening. Alex Lytle also went to Marjory Stoneman Douglas High School, and she put her heart and soul into it. Now, we were doing this for all the right reasons, and we had talked to the families about it, but in the back of your head you're thinking, *If we screw up even an eyelash on one of these beautiful children, then it doesn't matter if you get the other 16 right.*

There was that pressure, but we were also trying to put together the video commemorating the one-year anniversary. We were so worried about how to properly shape it. The vision we had was the phoenix rising from the ashes, and we so wanted to focus on the strong things that came out of this, and that no child's life was in vain.

At 5:00 PM we showed the video to the families, before the doors opened. I was in a suite with them, and I was going to see their reactions, in real time, to what we created. If any parent didn't like it, I wondered if they were going to turn around and punch me in the face. But we did it right, and they *all* appreciated it. It was very gratifying after. You do things for the right reasons, and usually it comes out the right way.

FRED GUTTENBERG
Shooting victim Jamie Guttenberg's father

To put it simply, I would describe Shawn as "big heart, empathetic, tough guy." When I tell you what it meant to me and my family—what it meant to my son and his healing—it was such a powerful healing time in our lives, when we really needed it. I can't stress enough how meaningful it was to us, and I'm just truly appreciative.

CHAPTER 20

CHANGING CAREERS

WHEN I TOOK ON AN EXECUTIVE ROLE with the Florida Panthers after my playing career ended, I had already developed a certain leadership style from my playing days, and I always wanted to hold people accountable. The Panthers felt that those qualities, much more than my hockey knowledge, could be invaluable on the business side of our operation. We certainly had no former players on the business side.

So when I was done playing, the opportunity presented itself, and I took advantage of that opportunity. And I can honestly say I'm still very happy with that choice. I think my wife's expectations of what I was going to be doing when I was done playing were probably a lot different than what the reality is. Unless you're actually around the business side, there is probably no way you *could* know how much is involved. I had somewhat of an understanding, but I don't think I really understood. It's a lot of work, and a lot of hours, but it's very fulfilling and I really enjoy it.

MATT CALDWELL
President and CEO, Florida Panthers
I thought Shawn might come in and help sell season tickets or sponsorships, but he's done so much more. He really works with every department;

he looks over marketing, public relations, communications, digital, all of our community efforts. He's done so much that we promoted him last year to chief commercial officer, which is a senior leadership position on the business side. Shawn's hiring has been a home run for the Florida Panthers. I joke with people all the time, when I introduce him to clients or to people in the community, to not let all the fights fool you. He *can* kick your ass, but he can also outsmart you!

We'll see where this road takes me, but I think I've always had the goal of being the president of an organization. If it turns out that I'm here in South Florida, in this role, for the rest of my career, I would be comfortable with that. I like the responsibility that I have, I like my relationship with our ownership group and the president and CEO, and I'm really happy where I am. I could see myself doing this for the next 15 years.

But I'm also a pretty aspirational person, and I always want to continue to climb the ladder. I want to take my business experience and continue to apply it no matter where I go or what I do. It doesn't matter if you're working for a sports team, a business, a private equity firm—no matter what it is. I think I could take this experience and apply it to other realms if need be.

BROOKS ORPIK
Pittsburgh Penguins

During the lockout, Shawn and I would take the train down to New York for negotiating meetings between the players association and the league. I got to know him so much better and learned there was so much more to him than what you saw on the ice. Just look at what he does now with the Florida Panthers. People probably assume that he's working on the hockey operations side of the business, but he's doing his work on the business side. I don't know what his education level is, but I also know that people who didn't get their degree are often very successful in their careers. Shawn was always very informed on the details of the negotiations. There was a big group of us skating every day at Boston University, and Shawn was always one of the guys who was very well-informed.

MARK RECCHI
Bruins teammate

What I learned over the course of two and a half years playing with him was that Shawn gets it. He's very smart, very astute. He's great with people, but he's also a leader. He knows the right time to take charge and the right time to back off. He is a great teammate and a great friend.

Believe it or not, I never had the desire to pursue management in the hockey operations end of the business. If I had an example of an ultimate goal it would probably be a role like Cam Neely's with the Bruins. Cam oversees both the business side and the hockey side, and someday I think I would love the opportunity to do something like that. I think I have some knowledge about the hockey side and what it takes to have a winning organization. I didn't know enough about the business side, and that was another reason why this opportunity was so attractive to me.

Don't get me wrong—I know I would have a ton of work to do to catch up on the hockey side of things, to get a better understanding of the players and salary cap implications. But I've been on winning teams, and I think I know what the DNA of a championship organization looks like. After playing for nearly 20 years, I *should* have an idea about that. But it's been the business side that I've really needed to learn.

Of course, no one in *any* business could have been prepared to deal with how our world—not just the sports world and the business world—would be affected by COVID-19. I had a discussion with my team about three and a half months into COVID, and I actually equated it, in a way, to the lockout. I certainly wasn't equating a bunch of millionaires sitting on the sidelines to a global pandemic, but hear me out on this one.

When we were locked out, I got up every day and I trained as if we were going to start playing the next day. Every day I tried to get a little bit better because I felt the end of the lockout was going to come someday, even if none of us knew *when* it was going to happen, or even if it was going to happen at all. But I would make sure to do something every single day that made me feel good about crossing that day off on the calendar.

I've tried to bring that same attitude here to this situation, and I try to make sure my people approach their jobs the same way. I tell them, feel good about yourself and your job when you go grab a beer at 7:30 at night. Make sure you feel good about crossing the day off, that you did something and didn't waste the day. I know it isn't always easy, and some days it sucks. But hopefully the hard work will make you feel better, so you're not just sitting on your ass feeling sorry for yourself. I want them to feel like they've improved, and their situation has improved, each and every day.

I have seven or eight direct reports to me in our management structure, and that means around 80 or 90 total people, maybe 100 or 110 if you include sales. I'm involved in everything on the business side with the exception of merchandise, food and beverage, building operations, and HR. I'm directly involved with ticketing, corporate partnerships, marketing, public relations, game presentation, creative, foundations, broadcasting, and community relations. I think that's everything.

I've played in some Original Six organizations where hockey is part of the fabric of the community, and it's not the same here in Florida. We're really in Ft. Lauderdale, not Miami, and we're working on a lot of the identity factors as we go forward. But make no mistake about it, we need to *win* here because we live and work in more of an "event" town. If we make going to a Panthers game an *event,* then people will come out to see us.

I had this discussion with the Buffalo Bills and Buffalo Sabres organizations. We're not a sports town, per se, but more of an event town, and Buffalo is just the opposite. Winning is just as important to them, obviously, but Buffalo is a *sports* town and not necessarily an event town. Boston is another town that lives and breathes sports every single day. I'm not sure it's the same here in South Florida.

When I was with the Blackhawks, we only had 9,000 people in the arena, and that's pretty similar to what we see here some nights. When I first got to Boston, that arena was half-empty a lot of the time. Then we took on the identity of the city, and the fans jumped back on board. But even in Chicago, there were some bad years.

To be a successful organization, you've got to work hard and set yourself up for when the team starts winning more consistently on the ice. You've got to be ready to pounce, make some noise, and grow your product and base. We are growing the game at the grassroots level, growing our base daily. One fan at a time.

You've got to work four times as hard for half the recognition, but that doesn't frustrate me; it makes me want to work even harder. Everyone on our staff here is of the exact same mentality. We don't control what is on the ice, and I'm very level-headed and even-keeled about that. I'm not out there on the ice anymore, so it doesn't affect my emotions like it did when I played. But we'll do everything within our power, on the business side, to make this franchise successful.

ZDENO CHARA
Bruins teammate, captain

Shawn is a very smart person. Sometimes it's very hard for someone to kind of feel or discover and learn or implement that skill and even roll it into the games. Shawn knew how to listen and learn. And he would implement

249

that into his role on and off the ice. He attended a lot of different events and contributed so much to the organization. But he made sure he talked to everyone; that's not comfortable for everybody. You know some people can be very comfortable in conversations with one topic and others with another topic. But Shawn could talk to anyone about anything. Politics, sports, workouts—you know, anything, He could talk to sponsors, different people, different business people. That's an incredible skill and obviously good for him because he's using that skill now with the position he has with the Florida Panthers.

I was accused of playing with my heart on my sleeve, but I think I left it there when I hung up my skates. I never understood how coaches who had played before could be so monotone and even-keeled when there was a penalty or something went bad on the ice. And with some of those coaches, you literally don't know what they're thinking. Now that I'm on the other side, I finally get it. When I stopped playing, all of that just left me. I don't know how to explain it, but it's just gone.

When I played my last game in the NHL I literally threw my skates into the garbage can, but our trainer pulled them out. He said, "I got these out, in case you ever want them again." I ended up auctioning them off to benefit the foundation, and someone paid something like $2,500 and he has my last pair of skates.

Unfortunately, I've had to pull skates back on a few times. Once was for a charity game, once for a skating event for one of our team doctors, and a few times with my daughter who can actually skate pretty well now. I'm the world's best hockey dad. I just stand in the corner, drinking my coffee, and I don't say a word. The only thing I ask my daughters when they come off the ice is, "Did you have fun? Did you work hard?" I'm hoping not to have to go on the ice too often with my daughters. I'll leave that to their coaches.

EPILOGUE

PEOPLE WHO REALLY KNOW me know that I don't like talking about myself very much. When I played the game it was always about *we* and never about *me*. That's why Dale had to talk me into doing this book project. But when we decided to move forward, I made a promise to myself that I would be honest. I would tell the truth, as I saw it, and let the chips fall where they may. I like to think I was an honest hockey player, and I felt I had to be honest here too. That meant telling the whole story, and telling the truth—even if I didn't always look like the hero when I told it. I also asked everyone else who is quoted in this book to do the same thing. I'm grateful that so many were willing to do so.

But there was a bigger reason I eventually wanted to do this project. I wanted to serve as an example to young people out there. I wanted them to know that everyone has a chance to live their dreams, even if people are telling them they can't do it. Dale has a saying that he uses quite often—whatever you want most wants you. I feel like that's been the story of my life.

I was never the best player on any team I ever played on. Most of the time, I was probably the worst, at least in terms of physical ability. Many times growing up I was cut from the team before I even had a chance. But I didn't give up on my dreams, and I was willing to do

251

anything to achieve them. I was never willing to let others dictate what I could or couldn't do. That's the ultimate lesson.

I've also been so very lucky. I've been lucky to be able to play a game I love, and even make a living doing it. I've been lucky that many people saw what I could offer and gave me an opportunity to do so. I've been lucky that thanks to the Florida Panthers, I've been able to continue my career, and continue my growth, although now in a different part of the sports world.

I've also been lucky in life. I come from a strong family, and I've tried to pay that forward. When I go home to Erin, Nora, and Ainsley, I know what matters most to me, and I know why the years of struggle and effort have been worth it. I hope someday when my daughters read this book, they'll get a better idea of how their dad came to be who he is, and I hope to always continue to make them proud.

I have learned so much from so many—ownership, front office, management, coaches, teammates, trainers, equipment staff, and even opponents. I have so much respect for the people who make this such an incredible sport and who entertain so many people, every single season.

If you take nothing else from my book, please take this—never give up, never stop trying, never concede, never relent, never compromise, and never, ever stop fighting *your* way to the top.